MANY
ALARM
CLOCKS

MANY
ALARM
CLOCKS

SY SAFRANSKY

THE SUN PUBLISHING COMPANY

The contents of this book first appeared in *The Sun* in slightly different form.

Published by:
The Sun Publishing Company
107 North Roberson Street
Chapel Hill, North Carolina 27516
(919) 942-5282
thesunmagazine.org

Cover:
The Clock and the Blue Wing, 1949 (oil on canvas), by Marc Chagall (1887–1985)
Collection of Ida Meyer Chagall, Basel, Switzerland
Giraudon / Bridgeman Images
© 2015 Artists Rights Society (ARS), New York / ADAGP, Paris

Ordering information:
To order additional copies directly from the publisher, please visit thesunmagazine.org.

Library of Congress Catalog Card Number:
2014957472

ISBN 978-0-917320-17-0

Manufactured in the United States of America.

10 9 8 7 6 5 4 3 2 1

For Norma

Contents

Preface

I write in my notebook early in the morning, almost always before the sun comes up. (To the sun it doesn't matter, but it matters to me.) Some of the entries are long and carefully considered; some are just two or three run-on sentences: fragments of essays I'll never write, snatches of conversation, postcards from the dream realm.

Usually I write for at least an hour; on some mornings maybe a half-hour. Writing *something* every day is important to me — no matter how little sleep I've gotten or what mood I'm in. When I'm faithful to this practice, my skin has a rosy glow, the car starts in the morning, my cats come when I call. But I'm not always faithful. Sometimes I oversleep, or I wake up worried about an impending deadline and head straight to the office. Even then, I try to remember what the physician-poet William Carlos Williams said. He was also a busy man, known to compose poems between seeing patients. He insisted that "five minutes, ten minutes, can always be found."

I use a rollerball pen. I write on narrow-ruled paper. The paper is supposed to discourage big, loopy handwriting and keep my ego in check — a failed experiment, though I persevere.

For more than half my life I've lived in Chapel Hill, North Carolina. So, weather permitting and clichés about the South notwithstanding, my favorite place to write is in a wicker chair on the porch. Does it matter that I grew up in a kosher household in Brooklyn, New York — one set of dishes for meat and one for dairy; nonstop complaining in both English and Yiddish — and will never be mistaken for a Southerner, let alone a Southern writer? What matters is showing up in the morning. The Muse couldn't care less where I'm from.

Nonetheless, it's here in this Southern college town that I borrowed fifty dollars and started a magazine more than forty years ago. And it's here that *The Sun* continues to be published every month: an ad-free, independent journal to which I still devote most of my waking hours.

I used to write essays every month for *The Sun*. After all, one advantage of starting your own magazine is that, for better or worse, it gives you a place to publish your own writing. But here's the catch: if your magazine grows beyond your wildest dreams, you're likely to become a hardworking editor and publisher who can barely find time to write. (It doesn't help that I'm the slowest writer in the world; others may make this claim, but, trust me, I'm slower.) These days, instead of essays, I publish pages from my notebook.

Nine-tenths of what I write in the morning never gets into print because there's a thin line between being self-revealing and self-indulgent and, at least in broad daylight, I try not to cross it. But every month or so I type up the sentences that seem to have some merit. I edit. I edit some more. The words left standing are marched single file into a section of the magazine called Sy Safransky's Notebook.

That's where all the journal entries in *Many Alarm Clocks* originally appeared.

Many Alarm Clocks isn't a book in which you'll find any practical advice about how to start a magazine or how to run a magazine or how to circle the wagons in defense of the serial comma. Nor is this book likely to help writers who regularly submit work to *The Sun* and are understandably dejected over how many times they've been rejected, and who would like to understand why I'm so hard to please. My heart goes out to them, but I don't understand it either.

There's a lot I don't understand, as the following pages should make abundantly clear. In them I criticize my own writing and ruminate about love and loss, and faith and doubt, and hypocritical Republicans and feckless Democrats, and the wayward republic to which, hand over heart, I pledged allegiance as a schoolboy. I write about being a Jew who keeps a picture of a Hindu guru on his wall and sometimes prays to Jesus; and about being a husband and a father and, most recently, a grandfather; and about eating too much and about not meditating enough and about getting older every day no matter how many vitamins I take. Sometimes I talk to the dead. Sometimes I argue with God.

Though drawn from the magazine, *Many Alarm Clocks* isn't a random collection of Notebook pages. From more than two thousand published entries I selected those that best fit a handful of recurring themes, trying to avoid the temptation to make myself look wiser than I am, less afraid of dying, less afraid of living. Then I braided them together along a more-or-less chronological arc that begins in 2000 and spans nearly fifteen years. This last part turned out to be more challenging than I'd anticipated. If only I'd paid more attention when my grandmother, seemingly effortlessly, braided together several strands of dough into one magnificent loaf of challah. What would she have thought, I wonder, of that confused-looking man in rumpled clothes, his hair disheveled, pacing back and forth week after week in front of a wall covered with bulletin boards, compulsively arranging and rearranging more than six hundred three-by-five index cards, each with an individual journal entry on it?

Since the themes in *Many Alarm Clocks* repeat themselves, I sometimes repeat myself. For example, I often write about my wife, Norma, because, after having been married to her for more than thirty years, I'm still in love, and still regularly reminded how difficult it is to love another person the way she deserves to be loved. So there's probably too much arguing with Norma, and too much lovemaking with Norma, and too many references to the moonlight on Norma's long, dark hair. (As the poet Jack Gilbert wrote, "People complain about too many moons in my poetry. / Even my friends ask why I keep putting in the moon. / And I wish I had an answer.")

One of *The Sun*'s editors suggested that there's "too much about loneliness." I agree. What business do I have being so lonely? I'm a happily married man. I'd like an answer!

I also use the word *God* too much. (One hundred sixty-one times, God forgive me.) "There's a lot of coffee in this manuscript," another staff member said. "You could open up an espresso stand." There are two references to how many words the Inuit have for snow, two quotes by Eckhart Tolle, two quotes by Woody Allen, singing birds on page 62 *and* page 64, and *three* references to making love not war.

Though I tried to keep topical entries to a minimum, more than a few chapters are devoted to the terrorist attacks of September 11, 2001, and the misguided and shameful "war on terror" that followed. Because some *Sun* readers deplore my politics, and others wish I'd stick with the politics and stop obsessing about my so-called self, it's possible that some of you who plunked down good money for this book are going to be displeased. That's why every sentence comes with a money-back guarantee.

A note about how to read this book: any way you want, of course. This is still mostly a free country, unless the government has decided you're an enemy of freedom. You have the right to read back to front. You have the right to jump around, if you like jumping. But to avoid confusion I suggest you start at the beginning. Some of these entries were written by a middle-aged man who'd just gained a few pounds; some by a man in his sixties who'd just lost a few pounds. His president was George Walker Bush; his president was Barack Hussein Obama. His country was fighting one war; no, two wars; no, a never-ending war.

The title *Many Alarm Clocks* is purloined from the enigmatic spiritual teacher G.I. Gurdjieff, who maintained that most of us live in a trance state, a kind of waking sleep, but that it's possible, through a rigorous process of self-transformation, to wake up and discover our true nature. I don't presume to grasp the breadth and depth of Gurdjieff's teaching, and the jury still seems to be out on whether he was a great mystic or a great trickster, or both. But habitual early risers like me are sometimes tempted to claim the moral high ground and forget that getting out of bed is the easy part. So I value his reminder that "a man may be awakened by an alarm clock. But the trouble is that a man gets accustomed to the alarm clock far too quickly and ceases to hear it. Many alarm clocks are necessary and always new ones."

Just to be clear: I'm not a follower of Gurdjieff. *Many Alarm Clocks* isn't a guidebook to spiritual awakening. And though I read books by spiritual teachers, and sometimes interview spiritual teachers, and often describe my work with *The Sun* as "my spiritual path disguised as a desk job," I'm asleep much of the time, too. Every day I'm humbled by how challenging it is, during our brief stay on this mysterious planet, to wake up and stay awake.

Acknowledgments

Writers need editors. This is true, maybe especially true, when the writer himself is an editor. But just as doctors are notoriously bad patients, and a lawyer can be counted upon to be another lawyer's most difficult client, editing an editor can be a formidable task. So I'm grateful to my colleagues who rose to the challenge. Some proposed modest changes; others reached for a cleaver and asked for a little elbow room. If I'd accepted all their suggestions, *Many Alarm Clocks* might have been a better book. Still, more often than not, I swallowed the medicine, paid the fine, ruefully acknowledging that some heavily made-up sentence I'd once found so alluring wasn't doing me, or the book, any good.

I'm especially indebted to Luc Saunders, *The Sun*'s assistant editor, for his generous and insightful critique. I was, I admit, momentarily taken aback when Luc handed me his marked-up copy of the manuscript festooned with enough yellow, blue, and peach-colored Post-it notes to wallpaper a house. But after I'd broken the color code and studied his extensive page-by-page comments, I couldn't have been more grateful.

I'm also obliged to *The Sun*'s senior editor, Andrew Snee, for having no compunction about wading into a dangerously crowded paragraph, grabbing a rowdy sentence by the collar, and throwing it off the roof. Andrew's rigorous editing has improved the work of many writers; I'm fortunate to count myself among them.

Seth Mirsky meticulously proofread this book, as he

does every issue of *The Sun*, from his home in Maine. I thought of Seth when I read recently that bald eagles, who can spot a rabbit from a mile away, are making a comeback in his state. And it occurred to me that, notwithstanding an eagle's keen vision and razor-sharp talons, a rabbit in Maine is a hell of a lot safer than some obscure grammatical error trying to hop across Seth's desk.

When Carol Ann Fitzgerald, *The Sun*'s managing editor, joined the staff in 2013, I told her that, except for a few finishing touches, *Many Alarm Clocks* was ready to be sent to the printer. Then she discovered I'd been applying "finishing touches" to the book for more than two years. Were it not for her infectious enthusiasm and unflagging determination to move the project toward completion, the manuscript would still be sitting in my office, sighing dramatically every time I approached it to straighten a curl or trim a little more off the top.

I'm grateful to the Estate of Marc Chagall for permission to use his painting, *The Clock and the Blue Wing*, on the cover. Robert Graham, *The Sun*'s art director, is responsible for the book's understated and elegant design. For additional help, I'm indebted to editorial assistant Derek Askey as well as former staff members Erica Berkeley, Tim McKee, Lauren Holder Raab, and Angela Winter. Staff members Krista Bremer, Colleen Donfield, Rachel J. Elliott (who took the author photograph), Becky Gee, Holly McKinney, Molly Herboth, and David Mahaffey all contributed in their own way. And special thanks to my friends Heather Sellers and

Cary Tennis for their valuable advice.

To my father, my first editor, my toughest editor: my undying gratitude. And I bow to the cats who prowl the halls of this book. Nimbus and Cirrus are, sadly, gone, but Franny and Zooey are alive and well, and there's no mistaking their devotion to my writing as they lie sprawled across my desk, guarding my words, even from me.

Thanks above all to my wife, Norma, for the countless hours she put into this book. Norma works full time. She tends to her garden. She knocks on doors to get out the vote. There's yoga class, ballet class — she's a class act, my Norma. But she's never too busy to help me with my work. On an afternoon when she could be planting flowers up and down the Eastern Seaboard, she'll sit beside me, combing through pages she's read a dozen times before. And when she tells me to cut the last sentence of something — *the last sentence!* — she's always right.

Finally I want to thank you, the reader. We both know you could be holding some other book right now, written by someone wiser than I am — or, at least, more upbeat. Maybe you've made a list of all the books you want to read before you die, and you've fallen way behind, and this one isn't even on the list. But here you are, in a life too busy by half, about to take a chance on *this* book. Full disclosure: Someone who read an early draft suggested I call it *What Is the Sound of One Man Complaining?* She claims she was joking. Still, I thought you should know.

Let the Minutes Show

I WORSHIP ALONE in the early morning, my coffee as black as the sky outside. There's no rabbi here, no priest. No one is feeding me chicken soup for my soul. Here in the darkness, I won't be confused with a busy editor whose calls are screened, who gives generously to all the right causes, who every month assembles the wisdom of the ages on the last page of his magazine. Here, I remember that so many fools like me have come and gone. We eased out of bed before our wives were up, sat on the floor, talked to God. How skillfully we bargained. How beautiful our words.

LET THE MINUTES SHOW that I'm here, that I braved a none-too-happy childhood; legal drugs, illegal drugs; organized religion, disorganized religion; toothaches, stomachaches, the occasional headache, plenty of heartache; the death of my father, the death of my mother, the death of my infant son; three marriages, two divorces, and a long and utterly impractical love affair with myself.

MY FIRST CUP OF COFFEE must be strong because I want to be strong. This may be demanding too much of coffee.

My End of the Deal

HOW DID A NICE JEWISH BOY like me end up with such a stern Protestant work ethic? I take vitamins and go to the gym regularly. I defend the Constitution and signal before I turn. I'm in bed by ten most nights and up before five to exercise my right to be an overachieving American. Is this because I'm devoted to *The Sun*, or is it because I'm devoted to my own self-esteem? So who have I been trying to save with my Herculean labors: the world or myself?

PUTTING OUT *THE SUN* each month continues to be hard work. The long hours and the tough decisions sometimes wear me down. I'm not complaining, just observing — the way I observed how difficult it was to sit still at the meditation retreat last weekend. I was trying to follow my breath, but the pain in my legs was profoundly distracting, as were my wandering thoughts. I'll never learn to meditate perfectly. But I breathed in, I breathed out. I'll never learn to be a perfect editor. But I put out one issue, then another.

WHAT A BUSY DAY! I remind myself to savor it anyway. *This is my life*, I think, *not a dress rehearsal for some other life*. If, while emptying the trash, I notice how blue the sky is, then there's that much blue sky in my day: no more, no less.

SURE I WORK HARD. So do many other people. I try to remember something my friend Robert once said: "All those doctors who complain that they worked so hard in medical school — compared to whom? Someone who digs ditches all day? Someone who works back-to-back shifts at McDonald's?"

I TELL A BUDDHIST FRIEND that, no matter how hard I work, I never get to all the items on my to-do list. He nods sympathetically. Then, with a little smile, he asks, "Why not keep a not-to-do list?"

PUTTING OUT A MONTHLY MAGAZINE is my end of the deal: the covenant I make with God, or with my readers, and perhaps there's no difference. Maybe dreamers like me need a deadline the way the soul needs a body. Maybe we need to get roughed up regularly the way the immortal soul, in order to experience a human incarnation, needs to take birth in all-too-mortal flesh. The soul may dwell in eternity, but time has the last word here.

I WASN'T A REGULAR FOLLOWER of the *Peanuts* comic strip, yet I'm moved by the news of Charles Schulz's death. Here was a man in love with his work and the characters he'd created. In a career that lasted nearly fifty years, he never missed a daily deadline. He even had a clause in his contract dictating that the strip had to end with his death; no one could continue it. A few months ago, after having been diagnosed with cancer, Schulz announced he was going to retire. Last night, on the eve of the publication of his final strip, he died. His work and his life ended on the same day.

So Many Buddhas

IN THE SHOWER, the shampoo bottle falls and hits my toe. It hurts, but I don't bend down to rub it. I'm in a hurry. Later, at my desk, I'm writing out checks for Oxfam, Amnesty International, Seva. These modest donations are the least I can do. But I'm still in a hurry, annoyed at the time it takes to deal with the world's pain, too.

WALKING PAST THE UNITED NATIONS headquarters in New York City, I'm reminded that the UN is as old as I am. Since 1945, we've both been struggling with human nature. Yet how quickly I shut my heart to a disagreeable neighbor. How quickly I shut the door on myself! If I make a habit of judging myself harshly for every real or imagined failing, then how can I possibly extend generosity to others? My politics must be rooted in compassion for myself if I want to contribute to a more compassionate world.

ALMOST COMPLETELY PARALYZED by polio, Mark O'Brien spent most of his life in an iron lung. He wrote poems and essays and articles by tapping on a computer keyboard with a mouth stick. He was both an inspiration to me and a reproach, a fearsome reminder of how harsh life can be. I finally met him in person last June. (A month later I learned that Mark had died — alone, in the middle of the night, in his iron lung.) During our visit we talked about writing. We talked about dying. We talked about faith and doubt. I fed him a sandwich. I held a straw to his lips for him to sip some juice. Before I left, I wanted to hug him, but, of course, that was impossible. So I asked if I could touch his head. He said he'd like that. I told him I was glad we got to meet in this lifetime. He told me he was, too.

THE LAWS OF SUFFERING haven't changed, but every morning I stand before God and make my case. Yes, *that* God, the one with whom we're all on a first-name basis, whether we believe in Him or not.

I'VE TAKEN MYSELF HOSTAGE, Lord. Here are my demands: No more people I know being told they have cancer. No more guardian angels asleep at the switch. No more punishments handed down for crimes we committed when we worshiped the wrong gods; or when we thought that being in love would save us; or when we imagined, as smoke filled the crowded theater, that knowing where the exits were would save us.

WE LEFT THE TWENTIETH CENTURY behind. What choice did we have? The future beckoned with a new millennium, a fresh start. Yes, the century that gave birth to us was still breathing, but just barely. What were we going to do with a century that could no longer feed herself, or remember the difference between the First World War and the Second World War, or tell the Armenian orphans from the Vietnamese orphans from the Rwandan orphans? All the names of all her children, forgotten.

THIS IS THE FIRST DAY of the rest of their lives for the
360,000 human beings who will be born today. They've
come a long way for their precious incarnations. For them
we want to put our best foot forward; they deserve the best,
don't they? We're the caretakers — that is, when we're
not napping or watching television or going to war. Three
hundred and sixty thousand beings will cry today, the first
day of the rest of their crying. So many infants in so many
mangers. So many Buddhas opening and closing their
little hands.

Little Gentleman

I'M TOO SERIOUS. But I was always too serious. When I was seven years old, a relative called me a "little gentleman," and the label stuck. It made me proud at first, but as I grew older, I began to wonder: What did the little gentleman do to the little boy?

THE JESUITS HAVE A SAYING: "Give me the boy at seven, and I'll give you the man."

WE ALL CARRY THE PAST within us. Does it matter what we call it? I don't refer to the boy who lives inside me as my "inner child," but even if I did, would that make him any less real? When someone mispronounces "Safransky," does that make *me* less real? It rained all day yesterday. And all day the boy followed me, waiting for me to acknowledge him. But I was eating raisin bread. I was petting my cat. I was sulking because of something my wife had said. The boy looked at me. Maybe he was lonely. Maybe he was cold and wet. But I was reading manuscripts. I was surfing the Internet.

WILLIAM FAULKNER: "The past is never dead. It's not even past."

SOMETHING FRIGHTENED MY CAT Nimbus last night. I tried to soothe her, but she was still afraid. So I just sat with her, not trying to do anything, trusting that my being in the same room with her would help. Of course this is exactly what I need to learn to do for myself. My presence matters, even if at first I don't seem to be the friend I need.

TO REALLY LOVE MYSELF is a radical act. I don't mean self-flattery. I don't mean a pat on the back for a good day's work. I don't mean admiring the reflection of myself in someone else's eyes. To really love myself means to start with the naked infant: He has no name, no ideology, no ambition. He lies on his back, breathing evenly. His chest rises and falls. He's an animal who must be cared for by other animals. They must feed him and clean him and hold him. They must make sure he feels comfortable and safe, safe in their hearts. He's an animal who needs to be treated with dignity, even when he's covered in shit, even when he's crying for what he can't have, even when he's too much for his animal mother to bear. To really love myself is to start here.

I USED TO AVOID eating out with my mother because she'd complain about the food or insult the waiter. But in the last years of her life she became quieter and less argumentative. Even though she was occasionally confused, and struggled to find words and finish sentences, she seemed more peaceful. She expressed appreciation for little things, like being taken out to dinner. At the Chinese restaurant near the nursing home, I sat beside her. I fed her. The wontons glistened.

I'M LEARNING WHAT IT MEANS to *tend* to my feelings, to be tender with myself in the most fundamental way. This is where some healing can occur. It doesn't require getting to the roots of my sadness — though I can keep digging if I want to keep digging. I don't need to condemn my shovel or my small pile of dirt. But the story of my past is the story of my past: nothing less, nothing more.

Ties of Italian Silk

IN COLLEGE I WAS a political-science major who never took a creative-writing class. I went to graduate school to study journalism not because I wanted to be a writer but because I wanted to change the world. I didn't even start to write poetry or keep a journal until I was in my mid-twenties. That's when, on a beach in Spain, I took LSD for the first time, and saw the earth breathe, and discovered that everything was alive, and realized that if I wanted to report the biggest story of all — to describe not just the facts but the truth — I'd need to learn how to use a living, breathing language. Even after all these years, though, I'm hardly confident of my craft. Each time I start a new essay, I have to remind myself I don't write an essay by writing an essay. I write by putting down sentence after sentence: good sentences and bad sentences, handsome sentences and homely sentences. If the words are alive, my paragraphs don't need to show up wearing expensive suits and ties of Italian silk. Sometimes it helps to remember the poet William Stafford's advice: If you don't like what you're writing, "lower your standards."

I WANTED TO BE ELOQUENT, but Language was in one of her goddamn moods again, silent, brooding. I tried to touch her. She slapped my hand.

NOTE TO SELF: When the writing isn't going well, don't blame it on global warming or anti-Americanism or anti-

Semitism. Don't complain that with more people writing today, there must be fewer words to go around. Don't sign a petition that says the Muse is dead, or spread rumors about her temper tantrums, or try to cause a rift between her and the other goddesses. And when she finally staggers in, her hair unbrushed and her lipstick smeared, don't ask if she's been making out with younger, more handsome writers who know just what to whisper and exactly how to kiss her and who have made larger donations to her nonprofit foundation and, under the table, to her political-action committee. Don't ask if size counts.

I RECEIVED A WARM RECEPTION at my reading yesterday. It's gratifying to know my writing is appreciated; everyone loves the sound of applause. Today, however, I'm reminded of the Zen koan "What is the sound of one hand clapping?" When I'm writing in my notebook early in the morning, whose applause do I want to hear? If the words come from my heart, stripped of artifice and the need to impress, it doesn't matter. But when I try to make these sentences better looking, everything's lost. I didn't get up before dawn to watch a middle-aged man admire himself in the mirror. Is that a new shirt he's wearing? I'm not impressed. Naked, I tell him. Naked is all I care about. And I don't mean naked except for your underwear. And I don't mean naked except for your charming smile.

THE MUSE SMILES. *One more flight,* she whispers. I nod dumbly, too exhausted to reply. When she first invited me up to her room, I was a young man; I wanted to be a writer; I took the stairs two at a time. How many stairs I've climbed since then. How many times she's assured me there's just one more flight to go.

The Unfamiliar Bed

WHEN I FELL FOR NORMA, her name went up in giant letters on all the billboards along the road to my heart. I'd get up before dawn to write, then come back to bed a couple of hours later: a wake-up call she couldn't ignore. In the middle of the day, we'd meet at home — for lunch, ostensibly, though we rarely left time to eat. In the evening we made love before dinner or after dinner or sometimes during dinner, our bodies promising each other what bodies can never quite deliver, but we tried.

WHEN NORMA MENTIONED to our neighbor Manny that we'd be going away soon to celebrate our eighteenth wedding anniversary, Manny, who's been married fifty-two years, said, "It's a good start."

LAST NIGHT, MY MIND wandered. It wasn't Norma I was embracing, but the woman she was twenty years ago. We were burning up the sheets back then, every night a riot in the city, the two of us looting everything that wasn't nailed down. I wondered if the woman in my arms would be jealous. *Of course, you jerk*, said the woman in my head.

ALL THE THINGS WE COULD TELL the couple we were twenty years ago. All the things they could tell us.

MAYBE IT WAS THE UNFAMILIAR bed. Or the fragrance of a soap we'd never used before. Or the moonlight through the curtains. But making love with Norma in our hotel last night felt dangerously exciting, almost illicit, as if we were cheating. Hervé Le Tellier: "With a little bit of imagination, it is hard to be faithful, but with a huge amount of imagination, it may be possible."

DID I TALK TOO MUCH, taking advantage once again of Norma's seemingly endless capacity to listen to my seemingly endless thoughts? (Norma read this and said my thoughts aren't "seemingly endless"; they *are* endless.) It's a good thing I finally shut up and kissed her.

ANOTHER MISUNDERSTANDING with Norma — over nothing. Is it any wonder the world is filled with strife? All over the planet, people hate each other, kill each other — over nothing. We're all going to die eventually, but that gets forgotten. Norma and I forget it. The Serbs and the ethnic Albanians forget it, and the Israelis and the Arabs, and the Muslims and the Hindus. We're all married to one another, but instead of loving each other, we sulk, we grumble, we argue, we turn away. I say *we*, but I mean *me*. I'm the world at war.

IT'S TAKEN ME A LONG TIME to realize that the perfect partner — someone who shares my likes and dislikes, and who couldn't agree more with my political opinions and religious convictions and sexual preferences, and who'd never in a million years want to sleep with the window open when I want the window closed — doesn't exist. George Levinger: "What counts in making a happy marriage is not so much how compatible you are, but how you deal with incompatibility."

IN MY DREAM, our marriage was kept alive because every morning, instead of making the bed, I took the bed apart piece by piece, then put it back together.

NORMA AND I CELEBRATED our anniversary by going out to dinner. Then we stayed up late. What a pleasure to follow each other's thoughts into unfamiliar neighborhoods, then to chase each other's nakedness round and round the block. We fell asleep the usual way, Norma curled against me, the cats at the foot of the bed. At three in the morning, she woke up, violently sick from something she'd eaten, and spent the next two hours throwing up. In the bathroom, I knelt beside her, my arm around her shoulder. There are many positions for love.

The Weight of My Habits

EVERY MORNING, I WEIGH myself. Which God am I worshiping when I get on the scale? Sure, the body is a temple. But is 165 a more holy number than 175? It would seem so, from the way I worship. If there's more of me today, will God love me less?

AT THE AGE OF EIGHT, I went on my first diet. I lost twenty pounds, which I promptly gained back. I've been losing and gaining the same twenty pounds ever since. Even my forebears wandered in the desert only forty years. Haven't I learned by now that eating "comfort food" when I'm feeling lonely or sad isn't as comforting as tending compassionately to my feelings? But I forget this. I distract myself with overeating, then with the reformist zeal of a new diet. Oh, the weight of my habits.

WHEN I'M EMPTY, I want to feel full. When I'm full, I want to feel empty.

ACCORDING TO FAMILY LORE, I started out as a "bad eater" who needed to be cajoled into finishing my meals. Apparently my mother and grandmother were afraid I'd be just skin and bones if they didn't fatten me up. My grandmother had lived through pogroms in Russia; my mother had been an impoverished teenager during the Great Depression. I can understand their worry, misplaced though it was in a household whose cupboards were always full. I became chubby enough to suit them: "husky," "full-sized," all those synonyms for *fat*. But who makes me overeat now?

ALWAYS REACHING for the next bite instead of feeling fed.

I FASTED FOR THREE DAYS to remind myself that I can live with hunger. Now that I've started eating regularly again, can I remember that my hunger, like all my desires, is satisfied for only so long? Then it arises again, as insistent as ever: it's here when I sit down to eat, and it's here again a half-hour later, whispering in my ear. By eating a little extra today, I can't guarantee that I'll have enough to eat next week or next year. I can't bring back to life my Russian ancestors who waited in long lines for bread. Hunger, old friend, old enemy, old teacher: I can't vanquish you by overeating.

A Different Kind of Greed

HOW EMBARRASSING that I've figured out so little — about
how to run a magazine, about how to come to terms with
my intractable personality. Nor do I know how to come
to terms with the world's intractable personality. As I sit
here on my porch, drinking coffee, millions of people are
suffering. They are hungry. They are homeless. They, too,
have figured out so little, yet how many of them have the
luxury of sitting on a screened porch and writing about it?
All day, I get to wrestle with my feelings. Oh, the luxury of
tears.

I NEVER SAW MONEY as a symbol of personal power. Yet,
now that I have a few extra dollars in my pocket, I like
the expansive feeling that comes from spending a little
more on a bottle of wine or picking up the tab when I have
lunch with a friend. Surely it's not necessary to renounce
the material world in order to grow spiritually. Then I remember Gandhi's injunction: "Think of the poorest person
you have ever seen, and ask yourself if your next act will
be of any use to him."

I DON'T WANT A TAX BREAK. I don't want to get richer
while the poor get poorer. But I don't pretend this makes
me a saint, because I like what money can buy: a double
espresso, a room in a good hotel.

OUTSIDE, IT'S COLD AND DARK. Inside my warm, well-lit house, I'm finishing dinner. Being a man who takes so much for granted, I take this for granted, too. What blinds me to my great good fortune? Food and shelter, food and shelter: humanity's mantra for millennia, our unceasing prayer. How many of us have wandered homeless and hungry? How many of us are too weak to stand right now? In my mind's eye, I see a man no different than I am — except he's gaunt, starving, no roof over his balding head. I'm here. He's there. But because he's not here, he's less real to me than my cats, less real to me than the bills I paid this afternoon. I'm eating. He's hungry. I'm still eating. I've eaten everything on my plate, and I'm reaching for more. The food is so delicious that I just can't stop myself. More. Give me more.

HOW I YEARN TO BE a better man, though I know that's just a different kind of greed.

Nonjudgment Day

AFTER TALKING WITH MY FRIEND Tom about his newfound commitment to Buddhism, I was ashamed that I couldn't remember the last time I'd meditated. How spiritually inadequate I felt, like a boy who wasn't doing his homework. Every single day, the Buddha said, we should remember we're not here forever. Each moment is precious. So what am I waiting for? For tomorrow or the day after tomorrow in this disappearing act called a life?

IF I HAD TO EARN a living as a meditator, I'd be on welfare.

I PUT DOWN THE BOOK I'm reading, a book about mindfulness, and pour myself a cup of coffee. When I pick up the book again, I accidentally knock the cup to the floor. I realize, of course, what an opportunity this is for self-mockery. But would I jump in right now with a sarcastic comment if this had just happened to a friend? Can I simply be aware of what occurred without passing judgment? Living more mindfully means living more mindfully; it doesn't mean judging myself for not being more mindful.

SOMEONE SENT ME a bumper sticker that reads, NON-JUDGMENT DAY IS NEAR. It can't come soon enough.

TODAY, BEFORE DOING ANY of my practices, or not doing them, or agonizing over whether I should or shouldn't do them, can I just pause for a moment? Can I remember that I don't have to be perfect to experience a moment of perfect love?

GOD DOESN'T NEED ME to sing God's praises. God already knows all the tricks a man can perform with a twenty-six-letter alphabet.

DEEPENING MY AWARENESS is a challenge. It isn't a challenge because my parents didn't love me enough. It's a challenge because it's a challenge. I don't need to take it personally. I've spent years excavating my past, sorting and cataloging the wreckage. But who I really am, the essential truth of my being, can't be grasped by the mind, no matter how acute my insights. I've confused introspection with awareness, but they're not the same. Becoming the world's leading expert on myself has nothing to do with being fully present.

WHEN I DEPEND on what I know, I never get very far. As the meditation teacher Stephen Levine writes, "The mind creates an abyss, but the heart crosses it."

I'LL START WITH GRATITUDE. You can never go wrong with *thank you*. Since I woke up with a headache, I can be thankful I have a head. I can be thankful my head is where it belongs, that I'm a man with a head on his shoulders

and not up in the clouds. Does my head hurt because
I stayed up late last night drinking wine and smoking
marijuana with an old friend? Thank you for the vineyards.
Thank you for the seedlings, and thank you for the buds.
When I got home, Norma was sleeping. Thank you for the
moonlight on her long, dark hair.

The Towers Are Gone

I'M USUALLY OUT OF BED early. But on Tuesday, September 11, 2001, I just didn't want to get up. I slept past my five o'clock alarm. I slept past Norma's six o'clock alarm. I didn't wake up until 8:20, the latest I'd slept in years. As I shuffled to the bathroom, I recalled bits and pieces of the unsettling dream I'd just had. I was in a big city, its skyline dominated by a towering skyscraper. I heard a huge explosion and, looking up, saw the top of the tower enveloped by a mushroom cloud. I raced into the lobby to find out what had happened. People were running frantically in all directions. A reporter told me the explosion was the work of a religious cult. That's when I woke up. I had no idea what the dream meant. I took a shower and got dressed. I turned on the radio.

IF THE TERRORISTS WANTED to make a statement, why didn't they go on a hunger strike in front of the United Nations? Perhaps the example of Mahatma Gandhi or Martin Luther King Jr. wasn't inspiring enough. Why didn't they emulate the Buddhist monks who set themselves on fire to protest the war in Vietnam? Not dramatic enough; not enough pyrotechnics. If Tuesday's events seem like a bad movie, perhaps that's because Hollywood has convinced all of us, terrorists included, that the only way to get the world's attention is to blow up a building and make sure plenty of people are killed.

THE NEED TO FIND THOSE responsible for the violence becomes a war against terrorists, which becomes a war against terrorism, which becomes a war against evil. But who would wage a war against evil unless he's unable to see the evil in his own heart?

"THE WORLD," a radio commentator says, "will never be the same." I wonder how many times such words have been spoken. Were they uttered, with the utmost solemnity, after World War I? After the Holocaust? After Hiroshima? After the massacres in Tibet, in Cambodia, in Rwanda? The world hears the words. The world holds its bloody head in its hands.

AT A TEACH-IN a week after the hijackings, speaker after speaker condemned the terrorist attacks; then, with barely a pause, and considerably more fervor, each condemned U.S. foreign policy. I agreed with much of the criticism, but it seemed odd to revile the United States at a time like this. I wondered: To which other nations are we being compared? China? Russia? Great Britain? Japan? Where is the country that's done no wrong, the country without racial or religious enmity, the country that has always extended itself magnanimously to the rest of the world? Is it reasonable to expect the United States to love everyone unconditionally? Just how much unconditional love does each of *us* shine out each day?

NEVER HAVE I HAD so eerily prophetic a dream. Then again, on September 11, a curtain came up on a strange new world. A handful of terrorists, armed with nothing but knives and box cutters, brought down the tallest buildings in New York. In a country where size matters, the World Trade Center was a symbol of this nation's unbelievable wealth, its enormous power, and, let's face it, its manhood. Now the United States is going to war to avenge a wound that can't be healed. The people are dead; the towers are gone.

Even the Rich

NORMA IS IN NEW YORK CITY working as a volunteer for
the Red Cross. She's counseling those who lost their jobs
or their homes or their loved ones on September 11. Two
months after the terrorist attack, the mountain of rubble
that was once the World Trade Center still smolders.
"Ground Zero looks like a demolition zone," she writes,
"but then you remember it is a different sort of demolition.
One survivor of the concentration camps said the acrid
smell was horribly familiar to her."

SOME PEOPLE ASK: *How could God have allowed this to happen?* I wonder which God they're talking about. During
the most war-torn century in history, the one we've just
tossed away like a bloody rag, 200 million people were
killed. Which God allowed *that* to happen? A woman who
narrowly escaped death in the World Trade Center col-
lapse told Norma, "God must have been with me that day."
Norma replied that God was with the people who died, too.

I HAVEN'T SET FOOT inside a synagogue in years. Yet, like
many Jews, I wrestle with my God. I take personally
the suffering I see around me and don't understand how
a merciful God could allow it — as if God's mercy were
something I could understand. This God who destroyed
the world in a flood to punish humanity for being too . . .
human. This God who slaughtered all of Egypt's firstborn
sons to teach the Pharaoh a lesson. This Mother of All

Terrorists who lashes out with no warning. None of the people Norma spoke with got any warning. Now they're just barely getting by. Even the rich, Norma says, show up for their handouts. Even the rich didn't get a warning.

GRAHAM GREENE: "You can't conceive, my child, nor can I or anyone, the appalling strangeness of the mercy of God."

I WAS AGAINST the Vietnam War. I was against the Gulf War. But I'm not a pacifist. I'm grateful the Allies defeated Nazi Germany; they didn't do it with words. I'm glad a handful of passengers on Flight 93 fought the hijackers. Norma's commitment to nonviolence, however, is unwavering. Yesterday, after the U.S. started to bomb Afghanistan, she was in tears. "When is the right time to be a Christian?" she asked. "When Jesus said to turn the other cheek, did he mean only when it was convenient?" I knew the question was rhetorical, but I couldn't help myself. "What if Osama bin Laden were holding a gun to my head," I said, "and you knew he was about to pull the trigger, and you had a gun, too. Wouldn't you shoot him?"

Norma looked me in the eye. "Not even if he was holding a gun to your head."

I stared at her incredulously. "You'd let him shoot me?"

"No," Norma replied. "First, I'd try to talk him out of it. If that didn't work, I'd try to get the gun away from him. If that didn't work, if nothing worked, I'd put myself between you and the gun."

"THERE'S ONE THING a true pacifist and a suicide bomber have in common," Norma tells me before we go to bed. "They're both willing to die for their beliefs."

Give Me Back the War on Drugs

WHAT SHALL I PRAY FOR now? The triumph of good over evil? A better year for American business? Shall I pray to have more faith in George W. Bush than I did when he stole the election? I don't want to be fighting a war against terrorism. I want everything to be the way it was before. Give me back the War on Poverty. Hell, give me back the War on Drugs.

WAR: SUCH AN EASY WORD to utter. One syllable. It slices the air like a sword.

PEOPLE ASK WHEN we'll feel safe again. But, before September 11, we didn't feel safe because of crime. Because of AIDS. Because of kids bringing guns to school. Because the hole in the ozone layer is getting bigger and the rain forests are being turned into particleboard. Before the Soviet Union collapsed, we lived every day with the threat of nuclear annihilation. Did we feel safe then?

MAYBE SOMETHING in the human psyche has always needed a wolf at the door: If it's not blizzards or floods, it's terrorists or communists or Attila the Hun. It's the man next door who prays facing west, not east; who falls asleep laughing at Groucho Marx, not reading Karl Marx.

IS IT POSSIBLE FOR ME to feel compassion not only for those killed in the attacks but also for the terrorists, and for the angry Arabs who hate me because I'm a Jew and an American, and for the angry Americans who want to nuke Afghanistan? Who's to say how much empathy we're capable of? I've read of Tibetan monks and nuns, imprisoned and abused by the Chinese, who nonetheless regarded their captors with compassion rather than contempt; who saw them as misguided and ignorant rather than evil. The guards beat the Tibetans if they caught them praying; the Tibetans, even as they were being beaten, moved their lips in a silent prayer for peace.

The Hand That Writes It

EVERYTHING IS UNCERTAIN NOW; terrorism is a fact of life. But everything has always been uncertain. Could Osama bin Laden have dreamt up anything more terrifying than the truth of human existence, which is that we're all going to die one day? That's right: this form will be no more. The "I" who thinks this and the hand that writes it — gone. The man I've struggled all my life to figure out will have ended his struggle. Just what was the problem, anyway?

FREEZING RAIN SWEPT THROUGH the central part of North Carolina yesterday, coating trees and roads with ice. Bent by the weight, tree limbs snapped and fell, bringing down power lines. According to the radio, more than a million homes are without electricity this morning. *Thank God we're not one of them*, I think. At precisely that moment, our power goes out.

LAST NIGHT, WITH OUR POWER still out, the temperature dropped to the mid-twenties. Fully clothed inside down sleeping bags, we slept on the floor in front of the fireplace — which, like a sullen teenager, wants to be fed every couple of hours but gives precious little in return. Still, it's better than no heat at all, which remains the predicament of hundreds of thousands of families across the state. Norma is still asleep. Our cat Nimbus is curled up on the mantel next to the bronze Buddha. Cirrus, our other cat, is taking refuge in my lap. Knowing that the power will be back on in a matter of days makes the situation more tolerable. *It's temporary*, I tell myself. Then I remember that's true of everything: the blazing fire, our two cats, my lovely wife with the faintest whisper of gray in her hair.

THE WEEKEND IS TOO SHORT. Life is too short. Do I face that fact squarely, or pretend that I can trick life by hugging Norma more tightly and stealing one more kiss? Do I think I can escape my fate? I can't know how many more weekends we'll have together — only that the number is finite, and my appetite isn't.

GETTING UP BEFORE DAWN opens a door for me. Sometimes the door swings wide; usually it opens just a crack. Still, I'm grateful to be here — even though the darkness often makes me nervous; even though the loneliness is here with me, too. So I'm not so alone. There's the darkness; there's the loneliness; there's the clock counting off the minutes, reminding me that this life one day will end. If I get up early every day to pray and meditate, my life will end on a day I've gotten up early to pray and meditate. No protection there. Do I need protection? God comes as birth. God comes as death. Is the in-breath better than the out-breath?

TIME BRINGS OUT today's special. Every day it's the same routine. *You call this a meal?* I scowl. Time looks me in the eye. *Twenty-four hours*, Time says. *That's it.*

Just Drive

HAPPY BIRTHDAY, JOSHUA. No, I haven't forgotten. I still remember driving your mother to the hospital that day in 1972, frantic with worry, thinking, *This isn't supposed to be happening yet*, and I remember telling myself to stop thinking and just drive. I remember the long wait outside the delivery room — they wouldn't let me in — and I remember the machines that kept you alive, the blinking lights that kept blinking blinking blinking until, on the morning of the third day, they stopped. Thirty years, Joshua. And for all these years you've been a teacher for me, a different kind of teacher than the gurus from the East, with their accents and their robes; a different kind of teacher than my daughters and my wives and everyone else I've loved and been loved by. One day, you squeezed my finger with your little hand; the next day, you died. That's one lesson I've taken to heart, my crash course in impermanence. So I thank you, my teacher. Happy birthday, my son.

Her Cheek Is Still Burning

THE DALAI LAMA spends more than five hours a day in prayer, meditation, and study. But, he says, he also prays whenever he can during odd moments of the day, not only because it helps pass the time but because it assuages fear. He says, "I see no distinction between religious practice and daily life."

IF I PRAYED MORE CONSISTENTLY, would my prayers be more powerful, like the body of an athlete who works out every day? If I meditated more regularly, would I be more practiced at staying mindful during difficult times, instead of letting fear gobble me up? What a big appetite fear has. What a succulent morsel I was last night.

I PRAYED. It was a simple prayer. I prayed for the willingness to pray. Then I went running. I saw a car with a bumper sticker that read: JUST PRAY.

MY SISTER DROPPED A TEA BAG into a cup of boiling water she'd just removed from the microwave. The water shot into her face, scalding her with first- and second-degree burns. She's in a lot of pain, and called last night to ask me to pray for her. But to whom do I pray? To the same God who already knows she's suffering? To the God of first- and second-degree burns? To the God of light and the God of the thermonuclear explosion? Wasn't God guiding my sister's hand when she dropped the tea bag? Wasn't God guiding the pilot when he dropped the bomb on Hiroshima? My sister was slapped in the face and doesn't know why. Her eye is half closed. Her cheek is still burning.

REMEMBERING NOT TO LECTURE God when I pray.

WHAT'S HARDER TO FATHOM: the atrocities committed by the Nazis, or a prayer found written on a piece of wrapping paper in Ravensbrück, the largest concentration camp for women in Nazi Germany. The prayer asks God to remember "not only the men and women of good will, but also those of ill will. But do not remember all the suffering they have inflicted on us. Remember the fruits borne of this suffering: the loyalty, the humility, the courage, the generosity, the greatness of heart which has grown out of this. And when they come to judgment, let all the fruits which we have borne be their forgiveness."

I PRAY TO REMEMBER that God isn't my idea of God.

Enemy of the State

I DON'T HAVE AN AMERICAN flag on my car or my front door. But I'm more of a patriot than Attorney General John Ashcroft, who studies the U.S. Constitution as if it were a menu in a fashionable Washington, D.C., restaurant from which he's free to pick and choose. Is it an exaggeration to call *him* a terrorist? Dismantling the Bill of Rights is less dramatic than smashing a plane into a building, but more of a threat to democracy.

WHY ARE MOST ANTIWAR demonstrations so shrill, so self-righteous, so . . . warlike? On an unseasonably warm day in January, I stand on the National Mall listening to one interminable speech after another, feeling like an extra in a biblical epic with a cast of thousands, applauding at the applause lines, trying not to look bored. There are forty speakers on the program. Forty! Some of the speeches are thoughtful, even moving; most, however, are angry rants that ignore the sad lessons of human history. I mean, when have humans not fought with one another, or with Nature, or with their own natures? But I didn't come to Washington to be inspired. I came to be counted. Showing up for a march like this is the civic equivalent of washing the dishes or emptying the trash: the dirty, unglamorous work of living in a democracy.

WILL THERE BE A WAR with Iraq? Maybe, maybe not. But there will always be war — if not this year, then next year;

if not next year, then in five years or ten. Wasn't war in the headlines the day I was born? Won't it be in the headlines the day I die? It won't be the same war, of course. It will be fought with different weapons by different countries for different reasons. As always, history will be written by the victors. As always, the vanquished will teach their sons and daughters what they must never forget.

I WANTED TO BE DANGEROUS, an enemy of the state. But the state kept disguising itself as a midlevel bureaucrat with a bad case of hemorrhoids and a shaky marriage, a corner office with plenty of windows and two locked file cabinets where hundreds of people were buried, some of them still breathing when he told the gang with the shovels to cover them up anyway — just fucking do it and don't ask questions. He was going to call his wife now. They hadn't spoken since that stupid argument on the way to the airport. The traffic had been terrible.

I CAN CONDEMN Bush's politics without hating the man. It's no surprise that the president isn't more conscious. This isn't a very conscious society. I struggle every day to bring a little more consciousness into my life. Last year, Osama bin Laden was my enemy. Last month, it was Attorney General John Ashcroft. Last night, it was my wife. She wanted the window open.

Another Man's Joke

I CAN UNDERSTAND why Norma feels threatened if she thinks I'm attracted to another woman. I know how easily I feel threatened if I think she's attracted to another man. But when we try to talk about it, sparks fly and the lights go out. We sit in the dark, feeling helpless, staring at the frayed wires in our hands: red wires, green wires, blue wires. All those wires!

JEALOUSY KNOCKS. He wants to stay a few days. I try to explain that this isn't the best time for company, but he brushes past me, flops down on the sofa, plants his feet on the coffee table. *Now*, he says, *where's that pretty wife of yours?*

I'M GRUMPY BECAUSE NORMA had dinner last night with another man. I'm grumpy because it was dinner, not lunch. I'm grumpy because I shouldn't even care: they weren't fucking each other; they were just eating overpriced pasta in a trendy restaurant, just being friends. I'm grumpy because, after nearly twenty years of marriage, I'm still easily threatened by another man, even when the threat isn't real. My wife loves me dearly. She'd never betray me. Then why do I respond to every blip on the radar screen as if it signaled an attack? When it comes to marriage, I'm just like President Bush, insisting we need a $500 billion missile-defense shield to protect us while we sleep.

WE'RE FIGHTING A WAR against terrorism. But this morning I'm unaware of any threat to my safety except for the outfit Norma is wearing. I know she isn't looking for another lover; she just wants to show that she's still attractive. If only I were the kind of man who *wants* his wife to walk down the street in clothes that are sexy and revealing, who *wants* her to turn heads. But I'm not. I am, however, someone who understands that life is uncertain. What if this were my last day on this beautiful planet? Is this how I'd like to spend it, worrying that my beautiful wife was making herself *too* beautiful?

CLOSING THE NEWSPAPER, I wonder what unnerves me more: U.S. spy planes being able to decipher handwriting on a clipboard from an altitude of eighty thousand feet, or another man catching a glimpse of my wife's breasts?

JEALOUSY, OLD FRIEND, we used to spend a lot of nights together, telling the same old stories, the ones we never tired of repeating. I bought drinks, you bought drinks — what did it matter? We were the kind of friends who could finish each other's sentences. We dressed in black then. We looked so cool. These days don't you think we look a little ridiculous?

I HAVE MOMENTS of awareness. They're few and far between, but the hungry man in me is fed. How grateful he is.

Look at his face as he lifts the soup spoon with a trembling hand. *This is what I wanted*, his expression says. *This is all I ever wanted*. Then his wife laughs at another man's joke, and the spoon clatters to the floor, and the soup is forgotten.

They Wanted the Night to Be Over

THE DAYS GROW SHORTER. The old sadness returns, speaking a language I still don't understand. *Autumn*, I say, grateful to have a word for it.

I DIDN'T WANT TO GET OUT of bed this morning. I didn't want to get dressed, stick my head out the window, and wave to my readers. The sky was dark, of course; it always is when my alarm goes off at 5 AM. Rumors that the sun would soon rise swept through the crowd, but I knew this was wishful thinking. They wanted the night to be over, but I reminded them that, as usual, the darkness had other plans. They wanted me to say something upbeat and re-assuring, but I reminded them I wasn't that kind of man.

LONELINESS LIVES AT THE EDGE of town. I visit her now and then. Sometimes I bring a poem I've written, though she doesn't read much poetry. It makes her too sad, she says. My poetry, especially.

BEFORE I PUBLISHED the first issue of *The Sun* in 1974, I considered calling the magazine *The Sometimes Sunshine*. Given my melancholic tendencies, that might have been a better fit.

OK, LONELINESS, YOU WIN. Three wives: not good enough. Two adoring daughters: you didn't blink. Lovers, friends, two gray cats who sit on my chest and purr. You were napping, you said. You don't remember.

THE SPIRITUAL TEACHER Stephen Schwartz encouraged me not to try to explain loneliness, and not to condemn it, but to see it as a kind of prayer, a deep longing to feel God's presence.

I SIT HERE, waiting for God to appear, forgetting that God is already here, waiting for me. How easy to misunderstand, to imagine that God is a man: godlike, of course, but vaguely human. If I were a woman, perhaps I'd think God was a woman, too, with breasts as big as planets. Women with big breasts were never my cup of tea. But what a God that would be!

MY BODY IS THE TEMPLE. My marriage is the temple. My work is the temple. So sweep the temple. Worship in the temple. *Don't worship the temple!*

I WOKE UP THIS MORNING in a body, breathing. I'm drinking black coffee now. I'm still breathing. The dark morning stretches like a cat. The billions of people who are asleep are breathing, and the billions of people who are awake are breathing. How is it possible for me to feel alone?

The Day's First Mistake

SELF-IMPROVEMENT IS MY DRUG of choice, more seductive than marijuana, more addictive than coffee. But the idea that I'll be happier once I become a "better" man is an illusion. When someone I love dies, will it comfort me to remember that I went to the gym three times this week instead of two? When I die, will my daughters be heartened to know I was at my ideal weight?

THE CAT IN MY LAP doesn't care what I ate last night, or what I weigh this morning. She doesn't care what words I'm writing, or whether they're good enough.

INSTEAD OF WORRYING about how to improve myself, can I acknowledge that the game is fixed? My desire to be a better man and my harsh judgment when I fail to meet my lofty goals are two sides of the same coin: heads, I lose; tails, I lose. But Sy is an inveterate gambler. He still imagines that one day he'll win.

A FRIEND JUST RETURNED from a meditation retreat where the teacher posted a sign that read, DO NOT IMPROVE.

I CAN START THE DAY by criticizing myself for not having gone to sleep earlier, for having eaten that extra handful of nuts. True, true. But this kind of truth doesn't set me free. Why not be thankful, instead, that I opened my eyes and got out of bed? To take this for granted would be the day's first mistake.

YES, I DRANK TOO MUCH and smoked too much and talked too much. Do my transgressions rise to the level of an impeachable offense? If I'm going to be tried, I want a judge whose hair is unruly and whose suit is wrinkled, a judge who's occasionally been seen walking away from the courthouse with a joint in his hand. I want a judge who knows how to laugh; a judge who makes mistakes; a judge who knows that what distinguishes humans as a species is that, since the dawn of history, we've screwed up again and again. It didn't start yesterday when I ate from the wrong tree.

Charging the Matador's Cape

TOMORROW I LEAVE for a one-week vacation. This means that for the past few days I've had to work well into the evening. I know, too, that I'll need to work harder than usual when I get back. Scientists say that for every particle of matter there's a corresponding particle of anti-matter. I wonder if for every vacation there's an anti-vacation.

NUMBERS CALL TO ME. The phone rings. I'm surrounded by letters, manuscripts, bills. The work is important, but it's just as important not to lose myself in the work, in the higher realms of efficiency, in my little myth of progress. How easy it is to be a busy man: to sacrifice myself on the altar of accomplishment; to light the incense and chant the mantra of success — not for money or glory, but for success nonetheless. Theodor Storm: "I felt that tiny insane voluptuousness, / Getting this done, finally finishing that."

I RUSHED UP AND DOWN the aisles trying to cram as many accomplishments as possible into my shopping cart. Maybe tomorrow there will be a sale, and I can accomplish two things at once!

MY DAUGHTERS WORRY about me. They think I work too hard. Who can blame them? I *do* work too hard. I've been trying to get caught up at my desk ever since I started *The Sun*. The fact that it hasn't happened in nearly thirty years doesn't lead me to conclude it's impossible; instead I imagine

I just haven't tried hard enough. Like a stubborn bull, I keep charging the matador's cape — providing a lively spectacle, at least. Of course, my daughters see the sword hidden behind the cape. My daughters know that this performance can't go on forever; that one day the old bull will lower his head and paw the ground, not noticing that the matador's stance has shifted, his blade now extended, the peanut vendor in the stands yawning, ready to call it a day.

BUSYNESS IS A STATE of mind. I don't feel busy *because* I have ten things to do today. I feel busy because, even as I finish one thing, I worry about the other nine. Do I worry about having to breathe in and out all day? No, I just take one breath at a time.

AS WE LAY IN BED this morning, Norma asked what I was going to do today. "Save the world," I replied in a deadpan voice. "Did you say 'save,'" she asked, "or 'savor'?" I laughed. "Try 'savor,'" she said.

Dark Purple Plums

I ALMOST DIDN'T RECOGNIZE Norma in the fading light last night. I felt like a schoolboy who catches a glimpse of his teacher in an unfamiliar place. *That's her, isn't it?* he thinks. *In the next aisle?* Her cheeks are flushed, and she can't seem to make up her mind between the peaches, which look so ripe, and the dark purple plums.

MIGNON McLAUGHLIN: "A successful marriage requires falling in love many times, always with the same person."

GETTING NAKED TAKES TIME. At the end of a long day, there's barely time to step out of our clothes. But only when we're truly naked is the promise of sex fulfilled. No longer husband and wife. No longer Sy and Norma. The zoo gates flung open and the animals stampeding.

NORMA AND I LIVED on next to nothing when we got married. These days, there's enough to go around. Does that make a difference? It does. Is it an important difference? That depends. Back then, we took baths together almost every night. We talked philosophy. We fooled around. Our bathtub is bigger now. We still talk. We still fool around.

I'M MIDDLE-AGED, middle-class, no longer the long-haired young man who feared a few extra dollars in his pocket would corrupt him. My beard is gray. I have money in the bank, and my beard is gray. Before Norma and I made love last night, I took a little blue pill. I was a devil. I was a god. I was a miracle to behold. Just like the old days, when I wasn't so old.

NORMA AND I WALK along the shore, holding hands. The wind whips her beautiful long hair, streaked now with gray. Since we met, so many years have slipped away. Time: the punch line to God's favorite joke, one we never really get, though we smile politely and pretend to understand.

Only the Living Sleep

I HAD A HARD TIME falling asleep last night. The room was filled with moonlight, and my head was filled with thoughts about mortality: the mundane reveries of a middle-aged man. I thought about getting up to pray. Instead I went to the kitchen, got something to eat, and read the newspaper. This morning, I wish I had used that wakefulness differently. God was in the moonlight, and God was in my troubled thoughts. Illumination doesn't have to wait until I die. As Kabir said, all I'll have then is an apartment in the city of death.

I DREAMT THAT THE BASEMENT windows needed to be replaced because the wood was rotting. This surprised me: I hadn't realized I'd been living here that long. Then it struck me — I'm fifty-eight! — and I woke with a start. Maybe the deepest mysteries aren't those we've yet to discover but those we live with every day. These bodies — magnificent bodies — grow older. Now and then we check the foundation. Surprise, surprise: We live in homes that crumble. And we never know when we'll be summoned to get out of bed and leave through the nearest exit. No, we don't need to pack an overnight bag.

I HAVE NO PROBLEM acknowledging that there was an eternity of not-me before I was born. Why is it so hard to imagine an eternity of not-me after I die?

I DON'T NEED TO SEE death as an error. I don't need to re-
sent God for not creating a universe in which I live forever.
A Course in Miracles insists, "Nothing real can be threatened.
Nothing unreal exists." I've been trying to understand
those two sentences for twenty years.

AT HIS WAKE, Norma's grandfather was laid out as if
sleeping peacefully, but only the living sleep. We who were
still alive cried, joked, and breathed the same air — too
intimate an act to refer to in polite company, and before
the dead we're especially polite. But there we were, breathing in and breathing out, to honor this ninety-one-year-old
man who had outlived his wife by many years. He lived
alone right up to the end, never wanting to be a burden to
his children or grandchildren. One day he fell and broke
his hip; the next day, in the hospital, his heart gave out.
The doctors called the cause of death a heart attack, having no better way to describe what happens when a man
falls and doesn't get up.

A GENERATION OF MEN, wrote Homer, is like a generation
of leaves.

Five Hundred Years

IF I CARE SO MUCH about the environment, then why did
I fly to New York to visit old friends? When I checked
in to my hotel, the clerk asked whether I was in town
for business or pleasure. "Pleasure," I said, and the earth
whispered, *It's no pleasure for me.*

THE PROBLEMS JUST KEEP getting bigger, don't they?
When I was a young man, it was civil rights; it was an
immoral war being fought in a jungle nearly nine thousand
miles away. But even then, unbeknown to us, the planet
was getting hotter. Those hundreds of thousands of people
who drove to Washington, D.C., in 1963 to listen to Martin Luther King Jr.'s "I Have a Dream" speech, or, a few
years later, to march in antiwar demonstrations — how
much did they contribute to global warming? How about
the millions of people who drove to the first Earth Day
rallies in 1970? Talk about a carbon footprint!

Now that we better understand the scope of the problem, however, what sacrifices am I willing to make? Shall
I vow that I won't eat anything I haven't grown myself or
bought from a local farmer; that I'll bicycle everywhere
instead of driving a car; that, if I absolutely must fly, I'll
climb on the roof and start vigorously flapping my arms?
How about not printing tens of thousands of copies of
The Sun every month? But I don't want to complain about
global warming this morning. Instead I want to thank the
sun for shining brightly during some very dark years. I

want to thank the earth for how kindly she's welcomed us. Believe me, we didn't know it would turn out this way.

IT TOOK ME three years to find the right reading chair. Admittedly, I wasn't looking too hard. But three years! This makes it easier for me to understand why societies change so slowly. Sure, we can find the answer to some vexing problem: just give us five hundred years.

AS I EXERCISE, I listen to the news: another story about global warming. I'm sweating; the world is sweating. Are we strong enough to change what needs to be changed? I finish my push-ups. I wonder how many more I could do if someone put a gun to my head. Convince me my life depends on it, and suddenly I'm a little stronger.

She Drove All Night, She Says

"A HAPPY WIFE is a happy life," a friend tells me. There's no question that I'm happier when Norma's happy — unless her happiness involves going out of town without me. So I wasn't sure how to respond when Norma told me she was going to spend two weeks this summer as a Red Cross volunteer. On the one hand, I was grateful to be married to a woman whose commitment to helping others goes beyond lamenting how much suffering there is in the world. On the other hand, I didn't want her to go. Away. From me. I didn't want to confront the anxiety I experience whenever Norma leaves town. I need to remember that it isn't feeling lonely that's the problem; it's assuming that Norma's absence is the *reason* I feel lonely. After all, I can feel lonely when I'm with her, too. Perhaps I distract myself then by arguing with Norma, or making up with Norma, or making love with Norma. In Norma's absence, loneliness throws off its disguises and stands revealed: my constant companion for better or for worse, for richer or for poorer, in sickness and in health, till death do us part.

J. KRISHNAMURTI: "There is no escape from loneliness; it is a fact and escape from facts breeds confusion and sorrow."

SAYING GOODBYE TO NORMA wasn't easy. It never is, if you happen to be me. When Norma begins packing for a trip out of town, I feel as if she were also packing up the ground I walk on and the air I breathe. I know the anxiety

is irrational, that its origin is in the past — somewhere
between my mother's haunted psyche and the crib where
I lay crying, somewhere between her fear of men and my
outstretched hand. I've spent years in therapy gaining
more insight into this, but insights don't keep the panic at
bay. For a while I tried Prozac, a miraculous drug, as help-
ful as a raincoat on a rainy day, except I couldn't take the
raincoat off when it was sunny, and I had to wear it to bed.
These days I just accept the fact that before Norma leaves
town, I'm going to get drenched. I try to endure the racing
heartbeat and stomach-twisting dread without blaming
Norma for leaving and without blaming myself for feeling
left. It helps to remember that most of my anxiety will diminish once Norma is gone, since missing her always turns
out to be a different experience than *anticipating* missing
her. Being afraid of feeling lonely is what makes me panic.
Feeling lonely is just . . . feeling lonely.

LONELINESS IS HERE. She drove all night, she says, stop-
ping only for coffee and cigarettes. She had nowhere else
to go, she says. What difference does it make if my dead
mother told her to say that or if it was something she read
in *Psychology Today*? Calling her a liar never gets me anywhere. Loneliness takes off her coat, tosses it on a chair,
then curls up on the sofa as if she belonged here, as if I had
nothing better to do than to sit beside her tonight, just the
two of us.

I NEED TO REMEMBER that I deserve nothing: not Norma's smile and not the guarantee of another long weekend together. Not a good return on a safe investment. I don't deserve to be saved from my loneliness. I thought marriage would save me. It was an understandable mistake.

I Argued with a Box of Crackers

AT NIGHT, MY APPETITE is a mob that wants it all. It's
ready to burn a few buildings, loot and pillage. Am I brave
enough to face the mob?

I LOST TEN POUNDS last fall, then gained it back. I guess
I need to hire an armed security guard to keep me out of
the kitchen at night — a square-jawed bully who won't
respond to my friendly overtures or laugh at my self-
deprecating jokes. I've been turning to food the way an
alcoholic turns to drink, the way a president turns to war.

MAYBE IT'S THE LONG winter nights. Maybe it's the
impending war. Gluttony laughs at me. *Go ahead*, he says.
Blame it on the season. Maybe it's all George Bush's fault.

I KEEP FORGETTING why I'm here. So I reach for comfort.
Maybe I'll find it in the bedroom with my loving wife.
Maybe I'll find it in the kitchen alone at night. Maybe I'll
distract myself with the world's troubles, read a newspaper
and eat some nuts. Have some more almonds, Sy. Have a
few dried apricots.

S.'S FRIEND HAS A SIGN on her refrigerator door: WHAT I'M
LOOKING FOR ISN'T HERE.

I MADE LUST THE ENEMY. I made gluttony the enemy. And,
day after day, my enemies won. This went on for many

years, because I was brave, because I was determined. What a brave, determined loser, my enemies agreed.

NORMA AND I ARGUED about — what else? — how we argue. After dinner, I argued with a box of crackers, and the crackers won. Oh hungry man, who neglects the only hunger that matters. Saint Augustine said, "Our hearts are restless until they rest in You." How important to be reminded that I'm hungry for something that food can't satisfy, that sex can't satisfy, that nearly thirty years of publishing *The Sun* can't satisfy.

Realm of the Fluttering Leaves

I DREAMT THAT MY dead mother told me she and I were
"still married" but "haven't had sex in many years." Is there
any hope for me, Dr. Freud? Being married to a psychiatrist hasn't seemed to help, nor have hundreds of hours of
psychotherapy. This morning, when I sat down to write,
my dead father pulled up a chair beside me; he wanted
to remind me I might not have what it takes to be a real
writer. And I wonder which of my dead ancestors I'll be
channeling at the staff meeting today, and why I worry
that some staff members only pretend to like me. Tell me,
little grasshopper: What is the sound of losing what you
never had? And isn't it futile, little grasshopper, to imagine
that an office full of happy, loving colleagues will ever
make the house you grew up in into a happy, loving home?

LAST WEEKEND, I heard poet and men's-movement-leader
Robert Bly tell of trying to get back home when his father
lay dying. In Seattle he missed a connecting flight. "Now,"
Bly said, his voice tremulous, "every time I'm in that
airport . . ." He started to cry, unable to finish the sentence.
Later, I told him how moved I was to see him weep in
front of more than a hundred men. He said it was easier
now that he was older; years ago, he couldn't cry even
when he was alone. But he went into therapy at the age of
sixty with a man who had a very expressive face. "I'd tell
him something about my childhood," Bly said, "and his
face would turn sad, and I'd say, 'Why are you looking so
sad?' And he'd say, 'What you're telling me is sad.'"

I TELL A FRIEND I felt abandoned as a child. *"Were* you abandoned?" he asks. I don't know whether he just wants the facts or is being deliberately provocative — drawing a distinction between someone who was emotionally abandoned and someone who was left on the steps of an orphanage. Suddenly I feel ashamed, as if I were making excuses for myself. Maybe I am.

MY LAMENT IS THE SAME lament. My wife is sympathetic, but she's heard it all before. Even the beautiful English language shakes her head when she sees me coming. *Him again*, she thinks, *with his fifty synonyms for sadness.*

WHAT IF PSYCHIATRISTS came up with different language to describe the suffering of people who troop into their consulting rooms every day? Instead of diagnosing a young woman with "borderline-personality disorder," how about "lost in the realm of the fluttering leaves"? Instead of "depression," how about "buried by avalanche, still breathing"? And, just as the Inuit have different words for snow on the ground and snow in the air and snow that drifts, maybe we could have different words for tears: tears we'll forget by tomorrow, tears we never cried but should have, tears that fall from our children's eyes, tears that fall too quickly to wipe away.

Dirty Little Secret

MY CAT NIMBUS IS ASLEEP on my lap. I'm in the lap of
luxury: black coffee by my side, strong the way I like it;
my notebook perched on the arm of my chair, which stays
rooted to this spot no matter where my thoughts wander. If
only my heart were as open as the arms of this chair. If only
my awareness were as steady as the legs of this chair. Even
George W. Bush could sit in this chair, and the chair would
remember to be a chair. Even Jesus, should he choose
to walk among us again, could take a load off. Go ahead,
Jesus. Kick off those sandals. Make yourself at home.

AFTER THE 9/11 TERRORIST ATTACKS, I promised to stop
demonizing our leaders. That's what al-Qaeda does, and it's
just a matter of degree. The president and I have much in
common, after all. Nearly the same age, we're both dili-
gent about exercising; both men of faith; both in love with
our wives. We're each, in our own way, engaged in a war
against evil. We're each, in our own way, deceive ourselves
about the progress we're making.

I'M GLAD I WENT to the antiwar demonstration, just as I'm
glad to be sitting here peacefully this morning with my cat
in my lap. But if a mouse suddenly darted across the floor,
how abruptly this peaceful moment would end. Could I do
anything to keep my cat from pouncing? Would it make a
difference if a hundred thousand mice had protested yesterday, chanting, *No more claws*?

GEORGE W. BUSH isn't the enemy. Human nature isn't the enemy. There is no enemy. Yet there is suffering. Gustave Flaubert: "Our ignorance of history causes us to slander our own times. People have always been like this."

OF COURSE POLITICIANS DISAPPOINT US. They're flawed human beings who pretend they know how to govern other flawed human beings. But we all know the dirty little secret, which is that most of us can't even govern ourselves. Not when we're up against the ungovernable nature of existence. Not when we remember what we try so hard to forget: the promises we've made; the promises we've broken.

I'M GRATEFUL FOR THE BIRDS who are singing this morning. Though I don't know what they're singing, I'm sure it's not a song of lament. Brushing my teeth in front of the bathroom mirror, I stare groggily at my reflection. *Yes*, I think, *that's me*, knowing the mirror would never lie, so I'm grateful for mirrors. Soon the sky will fill with light. I'm grateful for the light. I'm grateful for the trees outside and for their winding roots. They go down, down, down, so I'm grateful for darkness.

Rubble in the Square

WHEN I MARRIED NORMA, I was thirty-eight. I'd been married twice before. I'd done my homework, I thought. Yes, here in love's classroom, I was certain I had the answer. So why am I wearing the dunce cap again — the one that looks so cute on me, she says.

I DON'T WANT TO READ the words of Jesus today. I don't want to read the words of Buddha. Words didn't help last night when Norma told me how sad she was. I said all the right words. I know I did. Look at all my brave little soldiers, banners flying, rushing to the rescue, marching right off a cliff.

I WAVED THE FLAG of surrender. Not white enough, she said.

DO I PUT NORMA on a pedestal only to tear her down? It would seem so, from the rubble in the square.

YESTERDAY NORMA AND I talked about where to go for our anniversary. This morning, after another painful argument, I wonder gloomily whether we'll even feel like celebrating then. We have a travel agent. We have a marriage counselor. More than two decades in this house of marriage, and in some rooms we're quite at home, and in others we don't know whether to sit or stand.

HENRY DAVID THOREAU: "There is no remedy for love but to love more."

NORMA WANTED US to extend our trip another day. I didn't. But neither did I want to seem selfish, which is a pretty selfish motivation in itself. Our disagreement turned into an argument, not about whether we'd stay — nothing as simple as that — but about why, after all these years, we couldn't argue without hurting each other's feelings. Norma went to bed weeping. I lay on my back staring at the ceiling.

Happy anniversary, Sy and Norma. I guess you needed to be reminded that when you're celebrating a marriage, you're celebrating its difficulties, too. You're celebrating the fighting and the troubled sleep and the nights that last forever. And you're celebrating the sunlight coming through the blinds and the birds greeting the day. Are they singing for you, too? Impossible. But they are, you both know it, and you can't be too proud to admit it. The morning says, *Look, you're married to me, too*. The morning says, *Put on the coffee and start the day together, and start again, and start again*.

I DREAMT THAT I was dying. I was trying to figure out if I could transfer my frequent-flyer miles to my wife. I had so many of them — maybe enough for her to visit me. No, it turned out. She couldn't visit me.

On the Dance Floor

I TOOK MY VITAMINS. I prayed to the Four Directions. I deleted every e-mail the devil sent. But maybe I've got it all wrong. Maybe God doesn't care what time I get up in the morning or whether I was faithful to my wife in my dreams. Maybe God doesn't care whether I'm under a tree when lightning strikes or running across an open field. Maybe God doesn't care how many years I have left and whether I spend them wisely or bet all my chips on a risky hand. *Maybe you think the hand is risky*, God says, *because you want to win. Or maybe*, God says, warming to the subject, *you think I want you to win. Maybe you think I'm your steadfast ally, your silent partner, your oldest and most reliable friend. Maybe you think I want you to win for the glory of God. Think again.*

WITH THE DEATH of 150,000 people in the South Asian tsunami still dominating the news, I didn't feel much like celebrating New Year's Eve, but I kept my promise and took Norma dancing. I knew she'd been looking forward to it, and I remembered something a friend had once told me: his biggest regret, while waiting for the results of a biopsy, was not having danced more often with his wife. Out on the dance floor, however, I found it difficult to put the tragedy out of my mind. I reminded myself that more than 150,000 people die every day in this world; that Norma and I had made a donation to the relief effort; that here it was, New Year's Eve, and the band was better than I'd thought it would be. Later, we made love, waves of passion carrying us away.

THE DEATH TOLL from the tsunami has climbed to more than two hundred thousand, but a month after the event the story is no longer on page one — not in *The New York Times*, and not in the North Carolina press. Here, everyone is still talking about the traffic gridlock that followed a one-inch snowfall last week. As the snow quickly turned to ice, there were hundreds of auto accidents; drivers were stranded on roads for hours. "PARALYZED!" read the banner headline in our local newspaper the following morning, in letters not only bigger than the tsunami headline but, at one and a half inches, bigger than the snowfall itself.

Had the newspaper used the same formula to describe the wall of water that had smashed into dozens of coastal villages, that day's edition would have been impossible to print, impossible to deliver, impossible to believe. "IMPOSSIBLE!" the forty-foot headline would have read. IMPOSSIBLE! for the sea to be so ruthless. IMPOSSIBLE! for Mother Nature to be so indifferent. IMPOSSIBLE! for God to nap through it all in his La-Z-Boy, the remote in his hand.

Still, the suffering of those caught in a tidal wave doesn't diminish the suffering of those caught in a traffic jam. Suffering is suffering. A man stuck in his car is still a man, not a "harried commuter." Maybe he's on his way to visit a dying friend. Maybe he hates himself for having given in to some familiar temptation the night before. Viktor Frankl, the psychiatrist who survived three years in Auschwitz and other Nazi prisons, observed that a person's suffering is similar to the behavior of a gas: "If a certain quantity of gas is pumped into an empty chamber, it will fill the chamber completely and evenly, no matter how big the chamber. Thus suffering completely fills the human soul and conscious mind, no matter whether the suffering is great or little. Therefore the 'size' of human suffering is absolutely relative."

THIS MORNING, I MEASURED the little I know against everything I don't know. It was a useful exercise. It didn't take long.

MAYBE THE QUESTION ISN'T whether I believe in God but whether God believes in me. Am I the kind of man God would gladly introduce as one of his creations? Would I say the right thing, or blurt out something embarrassing about all the suffering in the world? The death toll from the tsunami in South Asia keeps rising. But I don't have to look at yesterday's headlines or peer into the unknowable future. Every day, thousands of people die because of malnutrition or disease or storms or droughts or fires or falls or pestilence or war. And those are just the human deaths. It's anyone's guess how many sentient beings are sacrificed on the altar of humanity's appetite for flesh or fur or cosmetics that don't irritate sensitive skin. Isn't it better to acknowledge suffering than to turn away from it — or, even worse, to try to make sense of it? C.S. Lewis wrote:

"Talk to me about the truth of religion and I'll listen gladly. Talk to me about the duty of religion and I'll listen submissively. But don't come talking to me about the consolations of religion or I shall suspect that you don't understand."

ALL DAY, I ARGUED against the existence of God. God didn't take my argument seriously. I built a home and didn't make a place for God. God followed me from room to room. I couldn't get away from this so-called God I didn't believe in. When I only pretended to pray, God wasn't fooled by my charade. I joined the hypocrites. I joined the holy ones. God waited patiently for my return.

History Sits at the Bar

I DON'T WANT TO READ the newspaper this morning. I
don't want to know how many people were killed yesterday to defend my right to call George W. Bush a killer.
The terrorists we've been told to fear are dangerous, all
right, but are they any more dangerous than the man
in the White House? On the fourth anniversary of the
September 11 terrorist attacks, I grieve for those who
lost their lives. And I grieve, too, for the way my country
has responded to that loss, like an angry man ripping his
neighbor's door from its hinges, then tearing the entire
house apart.

YES, IT'S TRUE: America isn't the country she used to be;
unhealthy habits take their toll. Tonight America sits in
her mansion, brooding. Her hair is wild; her robe is soiled;
the smell of death clings to her. She knows what they're
saying: Britain and Germany — even France, that hag-
gard slut — think they're better than she is. Why? Because
they've accepted the fact, or so they insist, that their best
days are behind them? *Well, fuck them*, she thinks, *and fuck
the lessons of history*. She stubs out her cigarette, stands
unsteadily, then squeezes into an outfit that's been too tight
on her since the end of World War II. Soon she'll be walking out the door with that little spring in her step that was
once the envy of the world.

LAST NIGHT I DREAMT that Saddam Hussein really did possess weapons of mass destruction. He'd hidden a nuclear bomb on the moon. If it exploded, the earth would be destroyed — and the weapon was set to go off soon. I notified the proper authorities, and disaster was averted. Maybe that's why I'm in a good mood this morning, even though it turned out the Bush administration had been right about *something*.

I TOLD A FRIEND I was still feeling aggrieved about last November's election. He suggested I take a more philosophical view. The ancient Chinese, he said, used to consider themselves fortunate if a great emperor came along once every five hundred years.

HOW EASY IT IS to keep up with current events these days, and how tempting, with so many sources of information only a mouse-click away. But all the screaming headlines will still be screaming their heads off the day I die — and no matter how many newspapers and magazines and blogs I read, I won't understand this mysterious world any better then. Meanwhile, History sits at the bar, raising his glass to whoever will pay for his next drink.

I'M GLAD MY CAT Nimbus doesn't start her day by reading about Shiite cats killing Sunni cats, or Palestinian suicide-bomber cats being mowed down by heavily armed

Israeli-soldier cats. I'm glad she doesn't listen to some cat on National Cat Radio telling her that everything that could have gone wrong yesterday did go wrong — while completely ignoring all examples of cat cooperation; cat compassion; cats making love, not war.

Three Days in the Wilderness

READERS SOMETIMES ASK how much I edit my own writing. I edit until each paragraph has lost the ten pounds it gained over the winter. I edit until each sentence can survive three days in the wilderness on its own. My father taught me to look at a sentence and, if it didn't deserve to live, shoot it between the eyes. Ignore the pleas of the women and children. Take no prisoners, he said.

WHY DO I IDEALIZE the Zen master who sneaks up behind a drowsy student and whacks him with his bamboo staff, yet fail to praise my father, who wielded his editing pencil and left some bruises, too? He also taught me to sit up straight. What better reason to bow to him?

NATURE, TOO, IS AN EDITOR. Isn't evolution a force that shapes all living things? It's no surprise, then, that the sentences we struggle to create must climb out of the muck, dragging their tails behind them. Stand up. Stand tall.

THE MUSE WHISPERS: Don't write like someone who fears death but puts a brave face on it or tells a self-deprecating joke about it; the world doesn't need another Borscht-Belt comedian. Don't write like a man who worries that his writing isn't good enough; is it good enough to tell your neighbor there's smoke pouring out of her upstairs window? Don't sit there coughing as her house burns to the ground because you can't think of a synonym for *fire*.

ANNIE DILLARD: "Write as if you were dying. At the same time, assume you write for an audience consisting solely of terminal patients. That is, after all, the case. What would you begin writing if you knew you would die soon? What could you say to a dying person that would not enrage by its triviality?"

HELLO, DAD. I wonder what separates us these days: surely not this minor matter of which of us is currently breathing. Was I a good-enough son? I doubt it. Were you a good-enough father? Perhaps that's not for me to say. Your love meant so much to me when I was a boy. Imagining a world without you was like imagining the earth blown to smithereens and the sun extinguished. You were not only my father but my most demanding teacher, not only my most demanding teacher but my most trusted confidant, a man I loved and feared in equal measure. Well, Dad, let's meet here for a moment without the need to prove anything: two beings who walked side by side for a while in a world neither of us could comprehend, not that we haven't kept trying.

Zeus Showing Off

WHEN MY CAT Nimbus came in last night, she was wet from having been out in the rain. After I'd dried her off, she followed me to bed and curled up between my legs. Then, purring, she drifted off to sleep. I don't know who was happier: Nimbus at being comforted or me at being able to comfort her. This morning, when I woke up, I didn't want to roll out of bed and get right to work. I wanted to curl up between God's legs. I wanted a reason to purr. Then I felt embarrassed: Here I was, a roof over my head, food in the pantry, a loving wife beside me, my daughters both healthy young women. Here I was, my magazine thriving, my car running, my legs able to carry me up and down the stairs. What more did I want from the Merciful One? No more thunder and lightning? A promise I won't get wet?

LAST NIGHT, I CALLED J. We speak maybe once a year. I asked how things were going. He paused. His ninety-year-old mother had died last spring, he said. A week later, his stepson had been sentenced to life in prison for attempted murder. Then J. had discovered that the operation he'd undergone last year for prostate cancer hadn't been as successful as he'd hoped: there were signs the cancer had spread. For a moment, I didn't know what to say. J. laughed. I asked what was so funny. He said, "You innocently ask how I'm doing, and I tell you, 'My mother's dead, my stepson's in prison, and I have cancer.'"

ISN'T LIFE TERRIFYING ENOUGH without terrorists? Last night, I leafed through *The Merck Manual* — 2,655 pages of small type describing every last affliction to which the body can succumb. Better than any spiritual text, *The Merck Manual* reminds us of the nature of impermanence. One minute, we're healthy and strong; the next minute, something is rattling the door. We don't know what to call it, this new symptom that's suddenly upon us, holding a box cutter to our throat.

TODAY IS FOUR YEARS since the accident that nearly took my daughter's life; four years since the phone call that yanked me out of my Sunday routine, my idiotic notion that the day would go the way I wanted it to. It was a car crash. It could have been a bolt of lightning, Zeus showing off. It could have been an earthquake: Mara lives in Los Angeles, after all. Yes, it could have been anything. We open the cellar door, miss the top stair, and the floor rushes up to greet us. We remember to blow out the candle before going to sleep, but in the middle of the night the old wiring in the wall begins to smolder.

The force of the impact broke Mara's pelvis in seven places. It was months before she could walk on her own again. During her long convalescence, I sometimes wondered whom to blame for her suffering: Myself, for not having been a better driving teacher? Mara, for not being more careful? The auto industry, for not building safer cars? LA, for being a city in which people have to drive everywhere?

Of course, there's no one to blame — just as there's no way for parents to protect their children when they become young adults. How easy to fiddle with the radio and look up too late, or round a curve and not notice a sign we've noticed a hundred times before. "It's our knowledge of death that makes us pray," writes Michael Meade. "Every path a child takes looks precarious to the parent's eye. And it is, and *precarious* is an old word that means 'full of prayers.'"

I CAN'T KNOW what the next moment will bring — only that, whatever it is, it won't last. After all, it's not just this body that's impermanent. Not long ago, a fire ripped through the offices of a small magazine I admire. They lost everything: their computers, their desks, their chairs. But to live with the fact of impermanence doesn't mean worrying every day about the terrible things that can befall us. It simply means living with the knowledge that everything changes, *everything*. That's what life is; there is no other life.

Here in the Waking World

YESTERDAY NORMA AND I listened to a recorded talk about "enlightened sex." Then, last night, I dreamt that I was having an affair with another woman! After we'd made love, I looked at my watch and realized I needed to get home to Norma. The woman insisted on walking me to the train station so I wouldn't get lost. That's when I woke up. Goodbye, dream lover. Here in the waking world, I still remember how you welcomed me — in your narrow bed, in your small apartment, in the greatest city in the world. Here in the waking world, where I wouldn't betray my wife, I thank you for hurrying down darkened streets with me; for making sure, when I opened my eyes, I'd be with the one I love.

IT'S NOT JUST NORMA I'm married to, after all. I'm married to loneliness. I'm married to fear. I'm married to desire. I'm a devoted husband. I treat each of my wives with respect.

HOW DO I FATHOM the depth of Norma's love? There's the way she loves me when I've endeared myself to her — that is, when I've said or done something lovable. There's the way she loves me in spite of something I've said or done — that is, when I'm anything *but* lovable. And there's the way she loves me that has nothing to do with the kind of man I am, a love that embraces the very fact of my existence.

BEFORE LEAVING FOR THE OFFICE, I said goodbye to Norma with barely a glance in her direction. "Bye," she replied, not looking up from her desk. Halfway down the stairs, I stopped. I stood there, contemplating the tyranny of my busy mind, which always has an excuse for rushing, for trying to squeeze an extra minute out of the day. I thought about what I lose by not making every hello and goodbye more conscious. I shook my head. To let love die from a thousand acts of neglect — man, that's a funeral I don't want to attend. I bounded back up the stairs.

IN THE MOONLIGHT, I study the face of the woman I've loved for more than twenty years. I'm thankful the moonlight traveled such a vast distance tonight, just so I could see her sleeping.

Rumi Keeps Talking

THE FURNACE AT HOME isn't working. Fortunately it can be fixed. Unfortunately it won't be today, because a part needs to be ordered. So I'm sitting here wearing two sweaters, reminded not to take central heating for granted; not to take anything for granted, for that matter: a floor, four walls, a roof that doesn't leak. Last week, someone told me about *wabi-sabi*, the Japanese worldview that celebrates impermanence and imperfection: an old window made into a picture frame, an asymmetrical pot, a chipped vase. Norma and I hardly designed this house with *wabi-sabi* in mind, but since *everything* is impermanent and imperfect, the truth keeps poking through. The furnace is *wabi-sabi*. So is the armchair I'm sitting in. So is the man.

IF I REALLY ACKNOWLEDGED how little I know about the future, wouldn't I live more fully in the present? The truth is that I have absolutely no idea what's going to happen tomorrow. Life could take the most unpredictable turn. Tragedy could befall someone I love, or a tree could fall on my house, or some cherished belief could come crashing. A comet strikes the soft belly of the atmosphere, and the dinosaurs look up, amazed.

WHAT IF WE ACTED as if we had no future — not just because we might be dead tomorrow, but because the future won't really change anything? There are good days and bad days; they all end. Outer circumstances change, but the fact that outer circumstances change doesn't change. What life asks of us tomorrow won't be any different than what life asks of us today: to be here, now.

MY FRIEND DAVE delivers mail — the same route every day. Only the route is never the same. Each day he notices something different. "I want to be in *this* life," he says, "not doing something else while I'm doing this."

I'M STAYING UP LATE tonight, reading Rumi and drinking wine. Rumi is telling me there are hundreds of ways to praise God; what's important is to kneel and kiss the ground *now*. Probably, I should brush my teeth, go to bed. I should be like President Bush, who gets a full night's sleep no matter what. But Rumi is pouring me another glass of wine. Rumi doesn't care if I'm refreshed in the morning. Rumi keeps talking, and I keep listening, because somewhere a man my age is dying tonight, a man who was fit and healthy until six months ago, who rolled the word *forever* on his tongue like a grape his wife had peeled for him, as they lay naked beside each other, the night still young.

Bright Yellow Ball

MY DAUGHTER MARA has a suspicious lump in her breast; a biopsy is scheduled for later this week. If the lump isn't benign, then all my worries about being behind in my work and about the accelerated pace of global warming will have to move to the back of the bus. They'll need to pay attention to the sign that says, DO NOT TALK TO DRIVER. Those hairpin turns ahead, the sharp drop-offs on either side — won't I need to focus on them? Won't I need to figure out where the hell we are, and why the gearshift is grinding, and how to turn on the windshield wipers now that it's raining so hard?

A FRIEND I HADN'T SEEN in several years asked what my spiritual practices are these days. "Whatever they are," I replied, "they obviously aren't working very well." He laughed. He thought I was being modest, but I was just being truthful. After all, as I sit here reading about breast cancer — an unlikely diagnosis for a woman Mara's age, but also, unfortunately, harder to treat in young women — wouldn't I like to draw on some inner strength? Isn't this one reason I study all those spiritual books, and meditate, and pray: to be able to face tragedy and not flinch, to be ready for my own death or the death of a loved one? But keeping the anxiety at bay right now is like telling a drowning man not to panic. *The life preserver must be here somewhere*, the captain insists. *It didn't just get up and walk away.*

WHEN MARA WAS AN INFANT and would wake up crying, I'd wonder whether a dream had frightened her or whether she was frightened to find herself back in this dream we call the waking world. I'd hold her in my arms, trying to soothe her, telling her there was nothing to be afraid of: the oldest lie, the one every parent tells. Well, tonight I'm the one who can't get back to sleep. This means the gods can't come to me in a dream, so I have to call to them from this perch of wakefulness and hope they hear me. And if they do, what then? Should I get down on my knees, or face them with fists clenched, ready to rumble? If they want me to beg, sweet Jesus, I'll beg. If they want tears, I'll show them how a grown man cries. If they want a piece of me, a bloody chunk or two, no problem. *Hearty appetite*, I'll say.

I REMEMBER HOW I TRIED to bargain with God during the terrible arguments that regularly erupted in our house when I was growing up. As the yelling grew louder and my parents and grandparents exchanged ever-more-bitter insults, I promised God that, if he would make the fighting stop, I'd be willing to die ten years before my time — cowering behind the big chair in the living room, not yet ten myself.

WHAT DO YOU SAY NOW, God: my life for hers? I know, I'm old, twice as old as my daughter. Maybe I can bring something else to the table. Maybe your people and my people can work something out.

SY SAFRANSKY

ALL THE THINGS I HAVEN'T DONE for my daughters march
past like all the words I haven't written. They knock,
knock, knock, but I wasn't listening, too busy thinking
about whatever it was I can't remember. Life struts past.
Oh wow, you barely have time to say.

I'M ON THE STATIONARY BIKE at the gym when my cell-
phone rings. "It's benign," Mara says. I hop off the bike.
"Benign?" I shout. "Benign," she repeats. Tears and sweat
run down my face. *Benign*: such a lovely word. I want to
break into song. I want to kick up my heels. I want to keep
tossing the word back and forth between us like a bright
yellow ball on a sunny day.

In the Eyes of Gurus

HOW MANY TIMES have I prayed to see God? How many times have my prayers been answered? Still I'm unconvinced. When the bush burst into flames, didn't I turn on the radio to see if it made the news? Didn't I check the mirror to see if my beard was singed?

I SIT BESIDE A LAMP, not doubting the light it shines on this page. I don't say, *I believe in the lamp.* I don't argue with myself about what I mean by the word *lamp.*

WHAT WOULD IT MEAN to see God everywhere, even here in my kitchen in North Carolina? If I could see God here, I wouldn't need to keep looking for God in the eyes of gurus and between the covers of books. After dinner, I'd do the dishes, then step out on the porch and look at the stars. I wouldn't strain to see God in the distance.

MY FRIEND ROBERT doesn't like my using the word *God* so much. He's right. It's a blemish on the silence. Nothing can describe what's beyond description. But, as Krishna says in the Bhagavad Gita, "By whatever name you call me, it is I who will answer."

GOD: THAT HOLY WORD, that dirty word, that word we kill and die for.

I DREAMT THAT INSTEAD of worshiping one God, I was free to worship as many gods as I wanted. But I wasn't satisfied with the new gods I chose. I missed my old God, his self-assurance and occasional flashes of temper. My new gods seemed so eager to please. They spoke too slowly, too loudly, as if I were a foreigner asking for directions — not like my old God, who'd say, *Read the fucking map*.

Stale Wonder Bread

WINTER IS ALMOST OVER, and not a moment too soon.
These long nights stir up too many ghosts. But who am I to
question the movement of the seasons? My wish for some
kind of eternal springtime is laughable, like Bush's plan to
bring democracy to Iraq. As if we had a surplus of democracy here in the United States. As if all our democratic
institutions were humming along at peak efficiency, and
everyone's basic rights were being respected, and we were
all feeling so magnificently equal that we could afford to
give some of it away.

I DREAMT THAT I WAS READING aloud the names of young
men who'd been killed. I woke up weeping. "What's
wrong?" Norma asked. "I dreamt that young men were
being killed," I told her. "They are," she said.

THE PRESIDENT WANTS to spread democracy throughout
the Middle East like peanut butter and jelly on stale Wonder Bread. *Nothing wrong with these sandwiches*, the president
insists to the people of Iraq. *Most popular bread in America.
Just scrape the mold off and stop complaining. Or maybe you'd
rather be eating a shit sandwich at Abu Ghraib.*

IF TERRORISM IS A THREAT to democracy, so is errorism:
refusing to admit blunders; twisting other people's words;
consistently making statements known to be untrue. We
may never learn all the facts about George W. Bush's

presidency — whether, for example, in the months before 9/11 he deliberately ignored warnings about al-Qaeda because he already had his eye on Iraq and knew a terrorist attack would be a perfect opportunity to turn lemons into lemonade. What we do know is that the president seems to trouble himself with separating fact from fiction about as much as a suicide bomber, strapping on an explosive vest, worries about paying next month's rent.

WHAT IF EVERY POLITICIAN started speaking nothing but the truth? What if every one of us did? My friend Jim writes, "Isn't it odd that the hardest thing in the world is just to tell the simple truth? Without exaggeration. Without inflation."

BEFORE LEAVING FOR a local antiwar demonstration, I asked a neighbor how many years she'd been demonstrating for progressive causes. "More than sixty," she replied. Then she shrugged and added, "Not that it seems to have done any good." "Well, you never know," I told her. "If you hadn't demonstrated, things might be even worse." Did I really mean that, or was I merely trying to make her feel better? Perhaps I was just trying to keep my own spirits up.

BORN AT THE END of the Second World War, I grew up listening to my Jewish relatives condemn not only Adolf Hitler but every German who did nothing to prevent the extermination of millions of European Jews. What difference did it make whether ordinary Germans were privately revolted by the depravities of the Nazis, my relatives asked, if they did nothing to stop them? Well, the United States today isn't Germany in the 1930s, but I have a better idea now of what some Germans must have experienced as the Nazis began their rampage. How many suspected terrorists are being tortured this very moment by interrogators who claim to speak for me, an ordinary American, while I sit here petting my cat? If the interrogators were torturing my cat in front of me, I wouldn't just sit here writing about it. But they're not torturing my cat. And they're not torturing prisoners right in front of me, but in Iraq and in Guantánamo Bay and in dank cellars in Eastern Europe — far from where I'm sitting this morning, in this comfortable room with no blood on the walls, no screams echoing down the hall; far from this room where I read the newspaper and shake my head in dismay that somewhere a hooded man in handcuffs is about to be hit again. How vigorously I shake my head, thinking, *No, no, oh no.*

I Pick Up the Dictionary

MY FATHER WAS SIXTY when he died in 1974 — the same
year I started *The Sun*. I sent him the first few issues; he
wasn't impressed. Was this why I'd walked away from a
promising career in newspaper work, he wanted to know.
He was often dismissive and sarcastic when we disagreed,
which we did a lot in those days — arguments that left me
frustrated and tearful, though I wouldn't cry in front of
him. I'd wait until I was back in my car, then pound on the
steering wheel.

Once I asked him if he'd read any of the issues I'd sent.
He just waved his hand. "You're too much of an idealist,"
he said. "What's wrong with having ideals?" I shot back.
"Having ideals is one thing," he insisted. "Being impractical is something else." It was one of our last arguments. A
couple of months later, I sat beside his hospital bed as the
cancer that had ravaged his body for more than a year,
razing one neighborhood after another, bulldozed the few
proud houses that were left.

Today, only a few weeks shy of turning sixty myself, I
recall not just our irreconcilable differences but our incon-
testable bond. His temper notwithstanding, I never really
questioned my father's love for me. Nor have I forgotten
how physically affectionate he was, nor how funny, nor
how his judgment of himself as a "failed" writer has both
haunted and driven me, for better and for worse. On
impulse, I pick up the dictionary and look up *idealist*: "a
person whose behavior or thought is based on ideals; a

person who follows his ideals to the point of impracticality." What do you know, Dad? We were both right.

The Best Way to Worship Her

I READ THAT THERE'S ENOUGH lead in the average pencil to write fifty thousand words. Does that mean the words are in the lead? Of course not. Are the words in my head? Just where are they, those fifty thousand words?

THE GODDESS OF LANGUAGE laughs at me; she's amused that, after all these years, I still can't figure out the best way to worship her. Do I kneel before her with eyes open or closed? Do I sing her praises or keep my mouth shut? Today she whispers: Inside your head is an old wooden desk. There used to be an old-growth forest inside your head, but that was long ago. Now there's this desk, and a pencil, and a stack of paper — all made from the last tree on earth. You don't remember that tree, but it remembers you. Don't worry about the tree. Don't think about the forest that once stretched from one end of your imagination to the other. The world is different now. The trees are gone. Just pick up the pencil and write.

I SIT HERE WAITING for the perfect sentence to show up. But maybe the perfect sentence doesn't want me to wait. Maybe the perfect sentence is tired of one-night stands with writers who fall in love too easily, who can't be trusted to stick around when the perfect sentence turns out to be not so perfect after all.

FRUSTRATED WITH MY slow progress on an essay, I sigh. My gray cat Cirrus, perched on the windowsill, turns her head and stares at me with her limpid green eyes. Here we are, alive together, which her silent gaze expresses more eloquently than all my meowing.

TWO WEEKS OF WORK down the drain. I'm ready to strangle the man who claims he's a writer: he'll be dead, I'll be in prison, and we'll both be better off. Maybe I won't even be convicted. Maybe the jury will see it was a mercy killing.

WHAT DOES IT MEAN to ask for help with my writing? It doesn't mean asking God to whisper words into my ear. It doesn't mean lying down and taking a nap while he hunches over my laptop, fingers flying: *God, can he type.* The truth is, I don't know what it means. But I'm asking.

WRITE EVERY DAY, the Muse insists. Don't skip a day no matter how you're feeling, no matter how many wars your country is fighting, no matter how many tornadoes are heading your way. Crawl into your storm cellar and pick up a pen. If you can't think of anything to say, write the word *God* again and again. If you don't believe in God, write the word *dog.* Everyone believes in dogs.

Love with Its Fifty Exceptions

NORMA AND I CELEBRATE another anniversary, still in love despite our astonishing differences. Sometimes we're as different as night and day. Other times, the clock strikes high noon for both of us, and for a glorious few hours we're perfectly synchronized, as impressive as a Swiss watch, and a lot sexier. The mood doesn't last, but what does? Our marriage has lasted twenty-two years; still, I'd hate to be prideful. Who's to say love has kept us together rather than stubbornness or selfishness or fear of failing at love once again? The truth is that we have failed, innumerable times. How is it possible to love another person the way that person needs to be loved? Norma would be happier if I gardened with her. If I cooked more often. If I were a more involved stepfather. If I'd been more eager for us to have a child of our own. So pride would be misplaced here. But not gratitude. Gratitude we seat at the head of the table. We pour the wine. We serve the feast.

LOVE WITH ITS FIFTY exceptions, the type on the contract so small.

NORMA AND I AGREE that one of the strengths of our marriage is our ongoing conversation about the nature of reality. Some might call this "walking a spiritual path together," but that sounds sentimental and grandiose to me. After all, how many nights have I ended up sleeping on the sofa because one of our "spiritual" discussions got out of hand?

YESTERDAY, AFTER AN ARGUMENT with Norma, I understood exactly how it could have been avoided. But, as Fritz Perls said, "Understanding is the booby prize."

J. CALLS. He's in tears. At fifty-eight, he's been given the brushoff by his girlfriend. Later, I talk to L., who says he can't understand why, at the age of sixty-seven, he still can't find happiness with a woman. Did I once imagine that, as a man grew older, he'd become wiser about love? What an imagination! As for me, even after all these years with Norma, I'd be foolish to exaggerate how far I've come. A turtle, having walked halfway across the road, might think he's made some progress. And he might be right, so long as a car doesn't come hurtling out of the darkness, its driver humming along with the radio, his arm around his sweetheart. It's a love song.

A Man Who Forgot to Do Yoga

TODAY'S DATE USED TO BE important to me, but I can't remember why. Is it the anniversary of my first marriage? My second? Is it the birthday of an ex-lover? One who's dead, or one who's still alive? I feel as if I'm picking through the used suits at the thrift store, trying to find one that fits. What about this double-breasted pinstripe? But the jacket's too big, the pants too long. And, man, is it *old*.

JUST BEFORE MY SIXTIETH birthday, I was talking with a friend about the way we use language to deny the most obvious fact about old people: that they're old. Trying to hide one's age behind such euphemisms as "senior" or "the young old," I said, is like calling the death of civilians "collateral damage" or a used car "pre-owned." What's wrong with *old* — a simple word, honest and unadorned, that's stood the test of time? Old people might get more respect in this country, I said, if they respected the language a little more. My friend, in his late sixties, smiled and said he still calls himself "middle-aged." I paused, unsure how to get out of this tight parking space. "If sixty-seven isn't old," I asked, "what is?" He shrugged and said, "Seventy?" I told my friend I'd happily call him middle-aged if that's what he wanted. For myself, though, I'd be afraid of pulling a tendon if I stretched the adjective that far.

THIRTY YEARS AGO, if I felt tired in the afternoon, I blamed it on working too hard and not sleeping enough.

These days I chalk it up to being sixty. Is this ageism? I'm not sure. The truth is that I have slowed down. I no longer run every morning. I do fewer push-ups and sit-ups. My sister, Elyse, recently had knee-replacement surgery. It's not hard to foresee a time when we'll both walk, not run, to the nearest exit. Was this predictable? Of course. Did I expect that it would happen to us? Of course not!

IN YOGA CLASS, I LOOK at my tired, trembling legs, the legs of a man who forgot to do yoga for thirty years. "Don't forget to breathe," the teacher says. One more thing I've forgotten.

WHEN A TREE FALLS in the forest, do the other trees murmur, *It was such a young tree. It had so much to live for.* When it's finally time, I hope I don't take death as a personal affront, or blame the universe for making such a blunder. I hope I'll remember that the world will go on being the world without me, and without my attempts to turn my experience into language that will stand the test of time. And what kind of test is that, exactly? Time looks at me over the top of his reading glasses. *I guess you'll just have to wait and see*, Time says.

My Kind of Judaism

MAYBE I'D BE MORE optimistic about human nature if I
hadn't been born the same month Anne Frank died of
typhus in a Nazi concentration camp. Not long afterward,
most of the camps were liberated; newsreels in every
American theater showed bulldozers shoving thousands
of emaciated bodies into mass graves. As I was discovering what it meant to be alive on this planet, humanity was
discovering the new depths to which it could sink.

I'M A JEW who never goes to synagogue, who sometimes
prays to Jesus, who keeps a picture of a Hindu guru on his
wall. But last week, when Norma suggested that I trade in
my old Volvo for a more environmentally friendly car — a
used, diesel-powered Volkswagen or Mercedes-Benz modi-
fied to run on biodiesel fuel — I hissed, "Those are Nazi
cars." Maybe this is my kind of Judaism: to be kosher in my
choice of automobiles; to worship Volvos! Still, it's no joke
that Volkswagen and Mercedes-Benz not only supported the
Nazi regime during World War II but also used thousands of
concentration-camp inmates as slave laborers. And though
I'm not much of a Jew, I've never forgotten the Jews in the
camps; the Jews who, in their final moments, cried out not
to be forgotten by Jews like me.

NEARLY THREE THOUSAND people were killed when the
World Trade Center was attacked; to read aloud a list of
their names would take two hours. Six million people were
killed when the Nazis attacked European Jewry, reducing

it, too, to rubble; to read aloud a list of those names would take six months.

I TRY NOT TO PRAY to a sanitized God, an airbrushed God, the God of the silver screen. I pray to the God who put the green into nature and fire into the tongues of men; to the God of ceaseless change, who gives with one hand and smites with the other; to the God of the concentration camps and to the God of the bullies many of my Jewish brethren have become. I pray for the humanitarians and I pray for the barbarians and I pray to stop pretending I can always tell them apart.

NORMA AND I WERE INVITED to a Passover Seder. Norma, raised Catholic, had never been to a Seder; she was curious. I, the lamb who had strayed, went through the motions but didn't feel the Holy One. Later, when the conversation turned to animals, I started talking about my cats and how much they'd come to mean to me. How foolish I felt afterward, a Jew who loved his cats more than his own religion.

FIRST THERE WAS JESUS; then there was bingo. Moses brought the law to his people; then his people filed a brief with the court. We start with the shiny apple, then peel it and cut it and cook it and mash it. On the altar, we place a jar of applesauce.

He Who Killed the Bear

AFTER MAKING LOVE with Norma last night, I lay beside her, aware that my desire, so intently focused on her just minutes earlier, was now calling me downstairs for something to eat. Oh, this animal body, insatiable in its needs: *Fuck me*, it says. *Feed me*. Or, for a change of pace, *Feed me. Fuck me*. My appetites for both sex and food can seem insatiable, but I might as well complain that my appetite for breathing is insatiable. Is it shameful I'm such a hungry man?

DESIRE SAID, *Repeat after me*, and I did and I did and I did.

"I EXALT PASSION and pretend it's love," I tell Norma. "Even worse, I trivialize love and pretend it's passion." She says, "Yes, that way it's easier to bear."

LAST NIGHT I TOLD NORMA I didn't want to make love, then dreamt that I was chasing her all around Paris, unable to keep my hands off her, begging her to come back to our hotel room. She had places to go, she said, things to do. I, too, had places to go, I told her, and all the streets were named Norma, and they all led back to her. Later, I tried to undo the tiny buttons on the stylish new dress she'd bought. Ten buttons. Twenty buttons. Button after button from her neck to her ankles. How many buttons were there, I wondered. She laughed as I undid thirty more.

I LEARN TO UNDRESS HER, but not with my hands, not with my eyes.

I'M GRATEFUL THAT all my extramarital affairs occur in my dreams, and that most of them involve my wife. (Well, my *dream* wife.) I'm grateful, too, that even as a young man I realized that my attraction to women was unlikely to diminish as I grew older — in other words, that calling a man of sixty a "dirty old man" is no less a slander than calling a young man "dirty" because he'd rather spend Sunday afternoon reading poetry to his half-naked lover than watching football or figuring out how to get rich. The old man is dirty only if sex is dirty, only if the birds are dirty, and the bees are dirty, and the sweet honey taste of her lips is dirty. Sixty is dirty only if thirty is dirty. Dirt is dirty only if the planet Earth is dirty, only if God is dirty, only if children who sink their hands into God are dirty, only if the young boy surprised by his first erection is dirty, only if his covert glance at a young girl is dirty.

ONCE AGAIN, I DIDN'T sleep well. My wife was too warm, and the room was too cold. Norma is having hot flashes, which means she insists on blasting the air conditioner all night, so every morning I wake up freezing. I wonder if I should sleep downstairs on the sofa. I wonder if I should go to a motel. But I won't leave Norma's side, even though there are icicles in my beard. I won't desert my wife, even though she's single-handedly bringing on another ice age in North America. There's a huge white bear pawing at our window. Because I love my wife, I will kill the bear. I will wear its fur. I will be called He Who Killed the Bear for the Love of a Perimenopausal Woman.

The Crowded Tables of Café du Monde

HOW ARE WE supposed to understand You? You give
with one hand. You take away with the other. Let there
be light, You say. Let there be rogue black holes lurking
in the galaxy, swallowing stars that wander too close. Let
there be peaceful Sunday afternoons in the backyard. Let
there be noisy leaf blowers shattering the silence, and the
rockets' red glare, the bombs bursting in air. Let there be
a child learning to walk. Let there be an old man pushing
a walker, or being pushed in a wheelchair, or being turned
over in bed to have his diaper changed. So what will it be
today? Up or down? Boom or bust? Exaltation or disaster?
Heaven or hell?

AT THE GYM, climbing a staircase that goes nowhere, I
watched a commentator on CNN mourn the death of New
Orleans. And for the first time since Hurricane Katrina
had crashed into the Gulf Coast, I felt not only grief and
anger but also a pang of regret, because I'd seen many
great cities in my life, but I'd never seen New Orleans.
A friend once told me that New Orleans was one of the
most hauntingly beautiful cities in America: vivid, earthy,
sultry. Don't miss it, he said. And now, instead of picture-
postcard memories, all I have is a postcard from hell:
shameful, sickening images of people stranded with no
food or water, waiting day after interminable day for a
sign that they haven't been left to die.

THE TWENTY THOUSAND people trapped in the Superdome have finally been evacuated. But how many people will die around the world today of hunger and malnutrition? Twenty thousand. And tomorrow? Twenty thousand. And the day after tomorrow? Twenty thousand.

JOSH BILLINGS: "Remember the poor. It costs nothing."

THE POOR STAY POOR. The rich get richer. This is the land of the free, and you'd better be brave. And when God blesses America, make sure you're standing toward the front of the line, not way back in the barrios of New Mexico, or in a high-rise housing project in Chicago, or packed twenty to a room in a migrant shack in North Carolina. Make sure God spells your name right. Make sure you get a receipt.

RACIAL POLITICS HAVE BECOME more complicated than they were in the sixties, when I marched for civil rights. Yet my daughter Sara's decision to live in a predominantly African American neighborhood shows that racial politics can still be surprisingly simple. When was the last time I risked something for the cause of racial justice? I don't mean shaking my head at intolerance. I don't mean writing a check.

I PRAY NOT TO TURN my eyes from injustice; it's not the same old story. I pray to remember that thousands are dying today of hunger. My words don't feed them. I pray to remember the power of words, and I pray to remember their uselessness.

THOUSANDS OF PEOPLE have died horrible deaths. Does life go on? Life goes on. And one day the floodwaters will carry the rest of us away, too: black and white, rich and poor. Soon enough, we'll all be standing on the rooftops of our lives, calling to God to save us, surrounded by the crumbling levees we knew would never last. Soon enough, we'll all be gliding down the watery boulevards of New Orleans, swimming under the elegant balconies, darting in and out of the rusting streetcars, greeting old departed friends who've saved a seat for us at the crowded tables of Café du Monde.

YESTERDAY I OVERHEARD a man say that everyone gets worked up momentarily about a disaster of this magnitude; then, a few weeks later, we forget the whole thing. I wanted to object, but I knew it was true. Last December, all I could think about were the nearly 250,000 people who'd been killed in the South Asian tsunami. Now I can't recall the last time they crossed my mind.

Unknown Unknowns

AN ASTROPHYSICIST proudly asserts on the radio that scientists now have a "simple, well-defined model that explains everything in the universe" — or at least the 5 percent of it that can be described as "familiar matter." "Dark matter" and "dark energy," whose properties scientists don't understand, make up the rest. The radio show's host is incredulous. "Aren't we in the twenty-first century?" he asks. "To say we don't know what makes up 95 percent of the universe is astounding." I, however, find these numbers vaguely reassuring. Perhaps that's because, after all the years I've spent in therapy, and all the philosophical texts I've read, and all the spiritual teachings I've studied, at least 95 percent of my own existence remains utterly mysterious to me.

I CALL THIS LIFE *mine*, but do I own my life the way I own my house or the land my house is built on? Do I own the ground of my being?

SAY WHAT YOU WILL about Secretary of Defense Donald Rumsfeld, but his much-ridiculed observation in 2002 that there are "known knowns," "known unknowns," and "unknown unknowns" is sound epistemology. Imagine how much more gravitas his words would have had if uttered in broken English by a Zen *rōshi* with a shaved head.

IT'S ONE THING TO BE serious; it's another to be self-serious. Honoring the Mystery means being able to laugh at ourselves, too. Most of the great spiritual teachers have known this, I suspect. After all, how many people would have gathered to hear Jesus speak if he'd been just another self-righteous sourpuss? Clearly the man knew how to work a crowd. And once you have your audience doubled over in laughter, you can sell them the Brooklyn Bridge; you can convince them to love their neighbor.

I RARELY TALK in my sleep, but in the middle of the night my own voice woke me: "This is the Mystery," I said. Then, more emphatically, "*This* is the Mystery." And suddenly I was awake. And for a flickering moment I understood: The Mystery isn't out there somewhere, millions of light-years away. Nor is it waiting to reveal itself until after I become enlightened or, barring that unlikely possibility, after I die. Then, this morning, I came across these words by Ramana Maharshi: "God's grace is the beginning, the middle, and the end. When you pray for God's grace, you are like someone standing neck deep in water and yet crying for water. It is like saying that someone neck deep in water feels thirsty or that a fish in water feels thirsty or that water feels thirsty."

MAYBE GOD HAS NEVER BEEN as far away as I've thought. I can't say what God is. But when I stop pretending that I know who *I* am, God is here. When I stop insisting on my version of the truth, something reaches out for me: truer than any words, more luminous than any philosophy. This is something I've experienced, though I can't prove it. I can only honor or dishonor it by how I live.

Underneath These Clothes

MELANCHOLY IS BACK. She sits across from me, legs tucked beneath her. No, she says, she doesn't want anything to eat. The music I'm listening to is fine, she assures me with a small, sad smile. Yes, she's heard my favorite jokes before, all of them.

THE PHONE RANG at 3:15 AM — wrong number — and I couldn't get back to sleep. So I got up and got dressed. Before the sun came up, I'd read a stack of manuscripts, found a cure for cancer, and convinced Osama bin Laden to turn himself in. But I'm still sad. Go figure. You'd think someone as productive as I am could learn how to stop worrying and be happy. But the black dogs of depression keep nipping at my heels. Women haven't cured me. Sigmund Freud hasn't cured me. Nor have all the spiritual big shots I've met who've told me God is right over there; no, a little to the left; now back up a step; you forgot to say, "May I?" How did I get stranded here: sixty-one and counting, the windows of my mind covered with grime, a roof that leaks, a door that's coming off its hinges? A real fixer-upper, that's what I've become: just perfect for an elderly gentleman who isn't afraid of a little hard work.

DESPITE ALL THE THERAPY, and all the teachings, and all the legal drugs, and all the illegal drugs, I still don't accept myself. This, too, is hard to accept.

I DREAMT AGAIN of being in New York City. It's such a familiar dream, as if I'd never left. In the dream I'm alone. I'm lost. Sometimes I'm back in the neighborhood where I grew up, searching for a friendly face, but everyone's a stranger, so I just keep walking. Last night, I was looking at a map, unable to make sense of it. Maybe I need to pray for the Sy of my dreams to find what he's looking for. Or maybe he needs to wander because I've settled down.

LEONARD COHEN'S ZEN TEACHER told him, "The older you get, the lonelier you become, and the deeper love you need."

I'M CONNECTED RIGHT NOW to everyone who is reading this — more connected, probably, than if we were simply sitting in the same room. Yet I take the appearance of my aloneness as the deeper reality, imagine myself cut off, isolated. It's true that I'm the only person in this room, but I'm alone only if I ignore all the other people in all the other rooms, just because I can't see them, hear them, touch them. Connectedness is a fact I deny with my ideology of loneliness.

UNDERNEATH THESE CLOTHES, I'm naked. Underneath these thoughts, who am I?

I'M ALONE IN THIS BODY. It's the nature of an incarnation. The hand that holds this pen is my hand. These are my words. The fingerprints I've left on all that I've touched are unmistakably mine. The Japanese maple outside is connected to every living thing, *and* it's a solitary Japanese maple: one tree, distinct and beautiful. I can't love the world in the abstract, only in specifics. This tree. This cup of coffee. The rain this morning — a thousand fingers tapping, but not impatiently.

Objects in the Rearview Mirror

IT WAS A CHEAP SOUVENIR, a cast-metal reproduction, barely five inches tall. Still, I cherished my replica of the Statue of Liberty, which had the power of a religious icon in my boyhood home. My father's parents, who lived with us throughout my childhood, fled Russia in 1905 to escape poverty and the state-sponsored massacres of Jews, called pogroms. They told me about the elation they'd felt when, after an arduous three-week ocean journey, they'd glimpsed the majestic statue in New York Harbor for the first time. For them, and for a young boy brought up to believe in his country's moral supremacy, the Statue of Liberty was a symbol of refuge and hope. She was a gift from the French; her real name is *La Liberté éclairant le monde*, which means *Liberty Enlightening the World*. These days it's hard to say what she signifies. I just know my grandparents are gone, and so is my little statue.

THE HOUSE THE FOUNDERS BUILT is still standing, but there are cracks in the foundation, broken windows everywhere, and no more room to stack the dead. Let's face it: the house wasn't designed to accommodate hundreds of thousands of dead Iraqis and millions of dead Vietnamese, not to mention the ghosts of all the Native Americans and enslaved Africans who haunt the upstairs halls.

IT'S THE MIDDLE of the afternoon, and I'm tired. My country is dropping two-thousand-pound bombs halfway around the world, and all I want to do is lie down and sleep.

I'M THE GRANDSON of Yiddish-speaking immigrants. I've got an Eastern European surname I've dragged behind me all my life like a battered trunk from the old country. So when I read about plans to stem illegal immigration by building a two-thousand-mile wall between the United States and Mexico, I'm stunned by the lengths to which Americans will go to deny their immigrant roots, forgetting that objects in the rearview mirror are closer than they appear; forgetting that, except for those of us descended from indigenous tribes or from slaves brought here in shackles, we're all either immigrants or the children of immigrants or the grandchildren or the great-grandchildren or the great-great-great-great-great-great-great-grandchildren of some exile, some outcast, some stranger no one could understand. What a short memory we have. What did we name the children? Where did we park the car?

THESE DAYS, IF IT ISN'T my beloved's snoring that wakes me at night, it's my need to pee, or a dream about my dead parents or my ex-wives or the man I was half a lifetime ago: gone, gone beyond, gone beyond beyond, as the Buddhists say. Last night it was too much coffee. Then the frogs started croaking at two in the morning. *If this is their mating call*, I thought, *no wonder they're still frogs and not princes*. I turned on the lamp and read manuscripts. I would have preferred waking Norma and opening the book of love, but I knew she'd be less than enthusiastic about rereading one of our favorite chapters just then. Finally I turned off the light and tried to sleep. Moments later I heard two cats hissing and yowling. I ran outside to see our cat Franny squaring off with the neighbor's cat in a battle that was mercifully brief: no bombs dropped, no gunfire exchanged, no collateral damage except my loss of sleep. Back in bed, with Franny curled up beside me, I drifted off to the sound of her purring. I dreamt she'd been invited to appear on *Oprah* to discuss her new bestseller, *The Power of Meow*.

The Shape of the Barrel

I BROODED ALL NIGHT about a comment Norma had made, then curled up on my side of the bed, making sure our bodies didn't touch. This morning, I still feel angry. But why? I may as well blame the rain for falling, as if God owed me a sunny day. Let me get out the contract and take a look. Did God keep all his promises? Exactly which ones did I expect God to keep?

JOSEPH CAMPBELL: "Marriage is not a love affair. A love affair has to do with immediate personal satisfaction. Marriage is an ordeal; it means yielding, time and again. That's why it's a sacrament; you give up your personal simplicity to participate in a relationship. And when you're giving, you're not giving to the other person; you're giving to the relationship."

O GOD OF DROWNING SOULS, come to our rescue. Norma and I have gone over Niagara Falls in a barrel and still can't stop blaming each other. What is it this time? The shape of the barrel.

IT'S ILLEGAL FOR MY NEIGHBOR to blast his stereo in the middle of the night. But there's no law against my lovely wife keeping me awake. I try not to take it personally; it turns out that, for some women, menopause turns up the volume on snoring. *Menopause*: a word I used to ignore the way, as a vegetarian, I ignored certain items on the menu.

Who cared whether the pork roast had been marinated overnight or how much butter was added to the beef stroganoff? How little I understood as a young man about loving a woman as she grows older. It's two in the morning. There's a fat moon in the sky. I've retreated down the hallway to the guest room, where I lie on my back and stare at the ceiling, the kind of refugee I used to laugh at.

MY WIFE SNORES! My president lies! This isn't the America I was promised.

I GOT JEALOUS YESTERDAY listening to Norma talk about another man — how intelligent he is, how funny. He's just a friend, she insisted; there's no reason for me to feel threatened. But I did feel threatened. Did I trust that Norma was telling me the truth — or did I trust that she didn't want to hurt me by telling me too much of the truth?

WHEN THE RIVER OF TRUTH rises, when it washes over the sandbags I've placed around my life — for my own protection, of course — do I grieve or rejoice?

I'M NOT A HAPPILY MARRIED MAN this morning. I'm not a grateful citizen in the United States of Love. Go ahead. Tell me I live in the greatest country in the world. Remind me how many soldiers gave their lives to protect the freedoms I take for granted: my right to tell my wife she hurt my feelings; her right to remain silent.

A FRIEND CONFIDED to Norma and me last night that she loved her partner but wasn't sure she wanted to continue living with him. Wasn't it normal, she asked, to sometimes have doubts? Norma jumped right in. "Of course," she replied. "Everyone does." *Everyone?* I thought. "Sometimes I daydream about living alone," Norma went on, "in a place like Antarctica." *Antarctica?* My adoring wife fantasizes about a life without me in the coldest place on earth? No wonder I went to bed and dreamt I was in love with another woman. In a hotel room, shutters closed against the heat, we embraced in the fading light of a summer's day. In Africa.

Congregation of One

I'M HERE IN THE EARLY-MORNING darkness, a congregation of one. I'm here, just one more man who thinks he deserves God's ear, as if God had time for everyone who reached out. I'm here, reaching.

TO STAY ALIVE, do I need to understand the mystery I call breathing? Of course not; I just need to breathe. To pray, do I need to understand the mystery I call God?

I'LL NEVER BE an enlightened master or live in some palace of spiritual perfection. But if I can remember to be truthful and to keep my heart open, I can love the neighborhood I'm in. Maybe the wisdom I seek is closer than I think. Maybe it's as close as the hidden God, who doesn't shrink from the broken world, who doesn't abandon us even when we insist we've been forsaken.

I'VE BEEN AWAY from myself too long. Now it's hard to find the door. And when I find the door, it's locked. And when I knock, a hoarse voice answers. I ask him to let me in. He wants to know why I left. In that hotel room three thousand miles from home, was I closer to the living God, or was it God, too, I wanted a vacation from? Is that why I smoked so much and drank so much and ate so much? Is that why I didn't take a moment to sit quietly and pray?

I DON'T NEED TO WORRY that I've shut the door on God. God knows where to find me.

THY WILL. My will. Words make them seem different, just as *day* and *night* seem to describe two worlds.

GOD DOESN'T BLAME ME for laughing when I should have been crying; for wanting to kiss the girl and live forever; for hoping I could find happiness by some well-traveled route. God doesn't blame me for not knowing what God knows.

I'M SHOWN ONLY what I'm able to understand. Truth in all its glory would shatter me.

Feast of Feasts

I'M TRYING TO EAT more mindfully, attentive to each bite, no newspaper or magazine in front of me. Who knows what stories I've missed? Yet it hardly seems as if I'm neglecting what's important. Last night, eating a piece of freshly baked bread, I was reminded how shockingly intimate an act eating is. I was eating the body of the world — its fields of wheat, its fire, its salt — and, imperceptibly, my body was changing. One bite at a time, I was being nourished by something mysterious. I was eating rain. I was eating sunlight. I was eating a piece of bread and actually tasting it.

I WATCHED A FRIEND eat a cookie. Just one cookie. He took such small bites. Later, he said he "loved" cookies. Imagine that! A love that doesn't devour.

YESTERDAY, TO SLOW MYSELF DOWN, I imagined I was a condemned man and this was my last meal. Would I be in a hurry to finish? Of course not. So I paid attention to each bite, reminding myself that I *am* a condemned man, that this is it: this is the meal I came here for, feast of feasts.

"SELF-DISCIPLINE," my friend Robert reminds me, "is remembering what you really want."

WHEN I TOLD MY FRIEND DAVID that I was trying to eat more mindfully, he told me about the Zen student who was surprised to see his master eating lunch and reading a newspaper at the same time. "I don't understand," said the student. "You teach us to be mindful in all things. You say, 'When I eat, I eat. When I sleep, I sleep.'" The teacher replied, "And when I eat and read the newspaper, I eat and read the newspaper."

IF THE TERRORISTS WERE SMART, wouldn't they just encourage the nearly 70 percent of adult Americans who are overweight or obese to keep eating? Why strap on a suicide vest and blow yourself up when your enemies are already blowing themselves up with artery-clogging pizza and greasy french fries?

HERE I AM, ten pounds lighter than I was a month ago: my cat Nimbus on my lap, which probably feels the same to her; Norma insisting she doesn't care what I weigh; my readers unable to notice; the men in the locker room at the gym paying no attention. Even the mirror yawns. *You've got to show me something better than that*, the mirror says. *How about light pouring out of your third eye? Wounds where the nails pierced your hands?*

I Didn't Need to Shout

ONE OF MY NEIGHBORS has a bumper sticker that reads:
PEACE. Another has a bumper sticker that reads: WAR HAS
NEVER SOLVED ANYTHING — then, in smaller type — EXCEPT
FOR ENDING SLAVERY, FASCISM, NAZISM, AND COMMUNISM.
I've never been a fighting man. I didn't get drafted during the Vietnam War because I failed the physical. I had
something called a "pilonidal cyst." (You don't want to
know.) My deferment meant I didn't have to flee to Canada
or go to prison, because I had no intention of fighting in
a war that made as little sense to me then as the current
fiasco in Iraq does to me now. I've been a soldier only in my
imagination: as a young boy raised on movies about World
War II, I used to lie in bed at night and fantasize that I was
staving off waves of Japanese soldiers until my ammunition
ran out; then, under enemy fire, I'd crawl to a bunker to
retrieve more. These reveries ended when I discovered how
to masturbate. From then on, I fantasized about making
love, not war.

I DREAMT THAT I WAS the first bearded, Jewish, pot-
smoking leftist to be elected president. I demanded a recount.

I DIDN'T WANT TO GO to the antiwar rally last night; I had
too many things to do. But I always have too many things
to do. I asked myself: Am I really too busy to exercise my
right of dissent? *Use it or lose it*, Democracy whispered.

I thought about the antiwar movement. I thought about

how difficult it is to measure progress, individually or collectively, when it comes to social change. I thought about the first ten years of *The Sun*, when the magazine had fewer than a thousand subscribers and always teetered on the edge of bankruptcy. If someone had asked me then how much progress *The Sun* was making, what could I have said?

So last night I stood with the other protesters and said no to the war. I didn't need to hate. I didn't need to shout. I didn't need to pretend to be a better man than the ones who made the weapons or aimed the weapons. I just needed to say no.

WHEN THEY WERE YOUNGER, my two daughters argued incessantly. Their bickering frustrated me, but nothing I said seemed to help. One day a friend gave me some advice: "Don't say anything," he said. "Let them work it out. And don't keep insisting that they act lovingly toward each other just because they're sisters. That's your romance, not their reality." I followed his suggestion. My daughters didn't immediately stop fighting, but I think I became a more agreeable, more accepting father who didn't blame them when they didn't cooperate or insist that they be different than they were. Today, listening to the news, I realized that I react to humanity's familiar conflicts the way I once did to my daughters' battles. *If only my brothers and sisters were more loving*, I think. *If only they'd get along.*

She Was So Small

HAVE I BEEN A DEVOTED-ENOUGH father? When Mara
and Sara were younger, there were clearer benchmarks:
how much time I spent with them, whether I could provide
for their basic needs. Now that they're grown women, the
equation has become more complex. I wonder what they
make of me: a man whose approval is still important to
them; a man who sometimes treats them like children and
sometimes acts like a child himself; a man who, for all his
devotion, wasn't devoted enough not to split up with their
mother when they were little girls.

SARA LEAVES TODAY after a short visit. Meanwhile, I keep
staring at the headline — amazed at this most predictable
of stories, this miracle of transformation called "growing
up." Here we are, more than two decades after her mother
and I got divorced. The world ended then, but love survived. I never stopped being a father, and now both my
daughters are healthy, intelligent, beautiful women who
drive cars and pay taxes and make love with their boy-
friends and worry about the future and visit their father,
then drive away, fly away: they're here, then they're gone.
I'm sad that I see Sara and Mara so infrequently. It's not
the same sadness I felt when they were younger, and the
miles between us were a wound I thought would never
heal. The wound has healed. I run my finger over the scar
as I say goodbye one more time.

YESTERDAY, WHEN I RAN INTO a friend outside a local cafe, our conversation turned to world events. Before long, we sounded like two mourners at a funeral. His two-year-old daughter tugged at his sleeve. "Look," she said, pointing to a squirrel. We looked for a moment, then continued talking. A couple of minutes later, she interrupted us again. "Look at the cute squirrel," she said. I smiled at my friend, then told him I needed to go. I was a block away before I realized I hadn't said goodbye to his daughter. I had forgotten she was standing there, still entranced by the world around her. She was just a child. She was so small.

Reporting for Duty

PRIVATE SAFRANSKY reporting for duty, sir. Yes, I know I'm late again. I know that's why I never get promoted — that and what they call my "attitude problem." Yes, sir, I'm aware of my shortcomings — painfully aware, you might say, which is probably another reason I'm a sixty-two-year-old private and not a self-confident general atop his high horse. No offense intended, sir. Surely you recognize that I'm as committed as ever to the mission. When you remind us that a sentence should contain no unnecessary words and a paragraph no unnecessary sentences, I salute smartly. When you tell us we need to "show, not tell," I lock and load. When you order us to attack the enemies of good writing, I charge ahead. I may be an old private, sir, but I love my native tongue, and against her foes I take my stand.

REMINDER TO SELF: You don't need to sound smart, Mr. Smarty Pants. You don't need to have an MFA or a PhD. You don't need to know the answers to the ten most difficult questions. You don't need to know what those questions are. You don't need to make sure that everything you write is all muscle, not an ounce of fat. You don't need to send only your best and brightest sentences into battle. If you do send them, you don't need to pretend they'll win.

WHY DO I IMAGINE that my sentences need to be better dressed than I am? If I'm not the kind of writer I'd like to be, let me start with that. Let me start with my rumpled clothes, with the overcast sky, with how inadequate I feel to the task at hand. But, please, no more self-improvement schemes. The man I am is the man I am. As Paul Simon sings, "When they say that you're not good enough, well, the answer is you're not."

IN THE CARTOON, the psychiatrist tells his patient, "You have an inferiority complex." The patient asks, "What causes that?" The psychiatrist replies, "Inferiority."

THE INNER POET clears his throat. The inner poet insists that he can't begin working until the trash is emptied and the house is tidy and the planets are aligned. But there's no right time to start writing again. I can't wait until I'm enlightened. I can't wait until George W. Bush and Saddam Hussein sit down and work the damn thing out. As Gail Sher says in her book *One Continuous Mistake: Four Noble Truths for Writers*, "If writing is your practice, the only way to fail is not to write."

WHEN PABLO CASALS, the world's foremost cello virtuoso, was in his nineties, he was asked why he still practiced three hours a day. He replied, "Because I think I'm improving."

HOW CAN I MAKE SURE I get up early every morning to write? This is a question I ask myself every day, and the answer is always the same. It's a simple answer, but I don't want a simple answer. I want the answer to be long and nuanced, to take into account how little sleep I got last night, and how cold and dark it is this morning, and how my mother didn't love me the way I wanted to be loved. The answer isn't interested in all that. He's already up. He's dressed and waiting.

A Thousand Footnotes

ANOTHER SPIRITUAL BOOK. Another note in the margin. How many books like this have I read in my life? How many more am I likely to read? There's a breeze from the window. The woman I love is asleep beside me. The cats are curled at the foot of the bed. Turning the page, I wonder why I keep searching for truth in the eloquent words of others, as if truth were shy about appearing before me naked.

IT'S ONE THING TO ASPIRE to extend compassion to all beings. It's another to be concerned with whether others *perceive* me as compassionate. It matters to my ego, of course; my ego is eager to turn any selfless act into a photo op. My ego, you might say, is always running for reelection; no term limits here. My ego stays on message. My ego accepts cash, checks, and credit cards. My ego is always willing to make one more speech, shake one more hand. *No problem*, says my ego. *Leave it up to me, me, me.*

EVERY DAY MY EGO perpetrates the most egregious kind of identity theft.

I'M REREADING THE SERMON on the Mount. I could spend a year wandering up and down these winding streets. The streets appear ancient, but nothing is ever what it seems. Who do I think I am? A twenty-first-century Jew? A modern man with a laptop computer? And the poor, barefoot

Jew whom some called teacher: who was he? At the end of a dusty lane, I stop. I turn. If I raise my head just a little, I can see him.

GOOD FRIDAY, they call it. But isn't Good Friday the day Jesus was crucified? Why not Bad Friday? I guess it's good that Jesus allowed himself to be sacrificed for our sins — good for us, at least. Or maybe it was good for him, too, despite everything; maybe his crucifixion was the key to demonstrating that his teaching wasn't just words. His blood was real. His pain was real. At the end, did he really ask God why he'd been forsaken? Did he really expect an answer? If his flickering faith was part of his teaching, if his broken life was part of his teaching, then why should I look anywhere for inspiration but to my own brokenness? Why assume that his brokenness is holier than my brokenness, or less shameful, or less burdened with doubt or pride? Here they are, Jesus: a thousand footnotes attesting to my impeccable scholarship about the nature of suffering; all my canceled checks for all the books and workshops on how to be more spiritual — or, at least, how to look more spiritual; all my careful observations about what blinded me and what I could sometimes see. And when I could see clearly, I called it a good day.

THERE'S A ROMAN in me. He crucifies the Jesus in me. I must learn to forgive him. This is hard to do.

COLLEEN'S PARISH PRIEST says the most important part of Mass is the end, when he intones, "Mass is ended. Go now in peace to serve and love as Jesus did." Colleen writes: "I was thinking how different that is than just to say, 'Go now in peace.' It's like you can't have one without the other."

SURRENDER MEANS SURRENDER, not a dress rehearsal for surrender.

I CAN TRUST THE POWER of love. That's all I can trust. Not my story about the past; not my fantasies about the future; not all my remarkable insights, polished until they shine. They're like a wall full of trophies in a house that's burning. Better to trust the flames.

Heaping Spoonful

IN BED THIS MORNING, Norma seemed more interested in petting our cat Zooey than in wrapping her arms around me. So I felt hurt, and resentful, and after I got up I made a racket in the kitchen though I knew she was meditating upstairs. How little it takes to start a war.

THIS IS THE KIND of morning I'd divorce myself if I could. But what would I do then? Probably run out and find someone else with the same irritating habits, the same unfathomable anxieties.

ARE WE MORE MARRIED some days than others? It seems so. Does our marriage survive anyway? It seems so.

NORMA'S IDEA of a heaping spoonful is different from mine, so the coffee tasted watery this morning. She's more frugal than I am, which I admire, though I don't like watery coffee. Still, I don't need to criticize her. Nor do I need to see this as *symbolic*: She wasn't measuring out love. She wasn't reminding me I always want too much. We're just different, and our differences are married, too.

NORMA LOVES our new king-sized mattress. To me, it's as if we're sleeping in different zip codes. In the middle of the night, I hear her breathing. But when I reach for her, I can't find her. I drift back to sleep, remembering when I hitchhiked from New York to California in 1971, standing

at the side of the road with my thumb out, astonished by
what a big country this is.

WHAT RIGHT DO I HAVE to be here this morning? None.
No right at all. Yet here I am. All the more reason not to
take for granted my mysterious life on this mysterious
planet. My first cup of coffee. My next breath. Norma is
still asleep upstairs, although who knows where her dream
self has wandered: a thousand miles from here, a thousand
years. She was twenty-six when I fell in love with her —
that is, with her dancer's body, with her long black hair.
O shallow man. It wasn't until the first time I saw her
cry that I fell in love with *her*. Now she's fifty-two. There
are fewer tears. I'm still in love. And here come the birds:
always on time; always on key; always jubilant. At least,
that's how they sound to me. And what about the thousand
shades of green outside the window? This world would be
hard to believe if you'd never seen it.

The Story of Babar

MY DAUGHTER MARA is getting married next week — my daughter who is in her thirties now, not her twenties; not a teen; not a child crossing the street for the first time; not an infant I rock in my arms at 3 AM, too tired to think straight, the sleepless nights stacked up like planes in a holding pattern, the pilots growing drowsier and drowsier. Wake up! She's getting married!

MARA ONCE TOLD ME that before she reaches up to hug her six-foot-four fiancé, she sometimes hops onto a kitchen step stool to compensate for the height difference. Or they'll hug on the stairs leading up to their apartment, with Chris one step below her. This arrangement strikes me as not only eminently practical but also a wonderful metaphor for marriage itself, in which we're constantly called upon to raise ourselves up for another and also to humbly lower ourselves — not in self-abasement but in the spirit of forgiveness and love.

LIKE MOST BRIDES, Mara wanted a picture-perfect wedding. But with the economy sputtering, the war machine in full throttle, and the planet roasting on a spit, "picture-perfect" depends on how much we leave out of the frame. Even in the best of times, though, no one knows what the next moment may bring. We imagine our lives belong to us; from one breath to the next, I suppose they do. Seven years ago Mara was in a car accident that almost took her life; today, completely recovered, she's a radiant and elegant bride. At the end of the aisle, the tall, handsome groom is waiting. I give Mara to him, as if she were mine to give. He takes her hand, as if she were now his.

I DREAMT LAST NIGHT that my daughters were still young: Mara was four; Sara, two. I woke up in tears. How I loved those girls. How I love them still. Yet who they were at four and two feels closer to me this morning than this make-believe world of 2008. *"Scoot over here, girls, and I'll tell you a story." "About what, Daddy?" Mara asks. "About a long time from now," I say. "When?" Sara wants to know. "When you're thirty and Mara is thirty-two." They just look at me. "It's a story about ten thousand days from now," I continue, though I doubt they can grasp such a big number.* And for their father, too, it's almost impossible to imagine: a future in which we're not drawing pictures or playing Uno or curled together in the old *Sun* office on that worn-out, cut-velvet sofa reading *The Story of Babar* again, and again, and again.

TIME, THAT ILLUSIONIST, shows us there's nothing up his sleeve, and then, as if from thin air, produces summer, fall, winter, spring. Delighted, we applaud. Then, one by one, the places we've lived, the people we've loved appear from behind one curtain and disappear behind another. Amazing! Then, in the blink of an eye, we, too, disappear. How about that!

Forged Documents

RUNNING IN THE MORNING — thinking, as I often do, of how I might improve myself, live closer to my feelings, devote myself more completely to God — I'm stopped by two women, who want directions to a nearby church. Jolted from my reverie, annoyed that they've asked me rather than someone who is merely *walking* by, I tell them I don't know. They thank me politely; I run on.

It takes a minute for the irony to catch up with me, like a waiter chasing me with an unpaid bill: I was too busy thinking about God to help these women on their way to Him.

I'M A BEGGAR at God's doorstep, and I'm knocking, knocking, knocking. What if I'm asked to leave my rags at the door and come in? What will become of my rags?

THERE WAS A STORY about me in the newspaper. The reporter tried his best, just as I do when I write about my life. He didn't get everything right. But how much of the story do *I* get right? What if my reliable source isn't reliable?

"ALL THE INFORMATION I have about myself is from forged documents," says a character in the film version of Vladimir Nabokov's *Despair*.

AS LONG AS I INSIST I'm a separate *me*, how accurate can my story be?

DEEP DOWN, I KNOW that separateness is an illusion; that making "I" my central reference point leads only to suffering; that, despite the rational mind's inability to grasp it, all things are fundamentally joined. Unfortunately I rarely experience the world that way. Yesterday, however, while taking a walk, I became aware that everything around me, whether "animate" or "inanimate," was alive and aware, and not just a stage set for My Important Thoughts. I stopped identifying with my mind, and the incessant chatter I generously call "thinking," and felt myself part of a living intelligence that was more vast and magnificent than anything I could think about it. The moment came and went, as if I'd been kissed by an invisible lover, just a quick peck on the cheek before she slipped away.

WAKING UP IN THE MIDDLE of the night, I realize: as dreaming is to waking awareness, so is waking awareness to being truly awake. Then I fall asleep again!

I RECEIVED MEDITATION INSTRUCTION this morning from my cat Nimbus. First she tucked her front paws beneath her chest to demonstrate correct posture. Then she closed her eyes. She breathed in. She breathed out. *And remember to purr*, she purred.

Getting the Words Right

I HAVEN'T FINISHED even half the work I'd intended to
get done before leaving town today. I hope that before my
plane takes off, the pilot and the maintenance crew check
off all the items on *their* to-do lists. I hope that the baristas
in New York City have stocked up on coffee beans, and
the sanitation workers have picked up all the trash. I hope
that God, notwithstanding his considerable responsibilities,
hasn't fallen as far behind as I have, that he isn't keeping
millions of sentient beings waiting for an answer to their
prayers while he makes one last revision to the top of
Mount Everest and fiddles around a little more with the
Bering Strait.

WOODY ALLEN ATTRIBUTES his prolific output of one film
almost every year to the fact that he isn't like the characters in most of them. "I have a perfectly sedate life," he
says. "I wake up, do my treadmill, have breakfast; then I
write and practice the clarinet and take a walk and come
back and write again and turn on the basketball game or
go out with friends. I do it seven days a week. I don't travel
much. I could never be productive if I didn't have a very
regular life."

DUKE ELLINGTON: "I don't need time. What I need is a
deadline."

EVERY YEAR, NEW WORDS are added to the language
— too many, if you ask me. Nouns are dragged into al-
leys, beaten into submission, then sent back into the world
dressed as verbs like "transitioning" or "gifting" or, if you'll
pardon my English, "languaging." Marketers invent new
words to move more inventory. Specialists invent new
words to keep feeling special. My spiritually sensitive
friends invent new words to show how spiritually sensitive they are. Such people are likely to be surprised that
Ernest Hemingway rewrote the last page of *A Farewell to
Arms* thirty-nine times. When asked what the problem was,
Hemingway replied, "Getting the words right." He didn't
need new words to describe such fundamental experiences
as love and death and loss and joy, just as an accomplished
pianist doesn't need 96 keys or 110 keys; 88 will do just fine.

I DIDN'T FEEL LIKE WRITING today, but here I am, lacing
up my writing shoes. Here I am, lumbering around the
track. That's all it takes, the coach says. Just keep putting
one word in front of the other. It's not a race, the coach
says; no one is keeping time. Of course, we both know
that isn't true. No matter how fast I write, the earth keeps
circling the sun. No matter how fast I write, my pen will
one day run dry. Forget all that, my coach whispers. Forget
the ghost at the finish line, tapping his foot impatiently.
Forget your reader in the bleachers, yawning and checking
her watch.

AND STILL I BELIEVE in words: the right word, just one word, caked with salt and covered with seaweed, rising from the depths.

I'M TOO SHY TO WALK up to the English language and ask for a dance. She'd probably laugh at me — and who could blame her? Why would a gorgeous dame like her look twice at a lug like me? If only I were daring enough to take her in my arms, bury my face in her hair, and breathe in the words of the great poets. There'd be no need for me to finish a sentence, because she'd know exactly what I was thinking; no need to question her body pressed against mine, her long, lingering kiss.

Invisible Thread

AS THE ELECTION DRAWS closer, I don't know whether
we're heading for a crowning moment in American political
history — a gold-leafed invitation for dancing in the streets
— or an opportunity to discover how much lower the
United States can sink. Even if Barack Obama is elected
president, he may be unable to reverse this country's slow
and steady decline. Still, wouldn't it be something if he had
the chance? We know what can happen on Election Day:
not enough voting machines in predominantly African
American districts; improper purging of voter lists; votes
not counted or vote counts tampered with. Maybe the
terrorism-threat level will be raised to red the day before
we vote. Maybe the dog will eat the ballots. Still, wouldn't
it be something if the angelic host shone down on this
young and foolish country? Wouldn't it be something if this
fragile and wayward democracy could be set right again?

SOME OF MY FRIENDS worry that this presidential election
is our last chance for redemption; that if Obama doesn't
win, the world will end. But maybe the end of the world
has come and gone, and instead of acknowledging it and
bearing the pain, we distract ourselves with thoughts about
the future. For how many people did the world end in the
holds of slave ships? In the gas chambers at Auschwitz? At
ground zero in Hiroshima? In the jungles of Vietnam? For
how many people did the world end when the doctor told
them nothing could be done to save their child? The world

ended for the tens of thousands of people who died yesterday, and the day before that. The world ended for those who breathed their last breath certain they were seeing Jesus, and the world ended for those who died searching for a glimpse of mercy in the eyes of their executioner.

HENRY MILLER: "The world dies over and over again, but the skeleton always gets up and walks."

NO MATTER WHO'S ELECTED president, daffodils will bloom in the spring. Men and women will fall in love and, sadly, out of love. Inconsolable grief will still be inconsolable. A broken heart will nonetheless keep beating one hundred thousand times a day. No matter who's elected president, writers will write. Painters will paint. Three in the morning will still be three in the morning. The door in our psyche we don't want to walk through will still be just down the hall. No matter who's elected president, life will hand us the invisible thread that connects us all; love will hand us the needle.

My Inner Republican

IT DOESN'T FEEL RIGHT for Norma not to be here tonight. It never does. But I'm a modern man, married to a modern woman: she drives to the airport, gets on a plane, and flies to a city hundreds of miles away. It all seems so matter-of-fact, so mundane, but not to the one inside, my inner Republican, who wants his wife home every night because his mother was home every night; who longs for a time when the planets revolved around the sun in an orderly fashion and the moon kept its dark side hidden. The one inside says goodbye to his wife, then wants to invade another country.

LONELINESS: MY FAITHFUL COMPANION. When I reach for her, she's always there. How readily she forgives me for all the times I've fallen in love, gotten married, left without a goodbye. With or without a ring on my finger, she knows I'll be back.

I LIKED OUR OLD DOUBLE BED. It seemed just right for two cats and their two humans. But Norma found it too confining, as if her dream-body were stuck in traffic on a crowded city street. She wanted spacious skies, windswept plains. Now we sleep on a bed fit for a king and as wide as America's fat ass.

WHEN NORMA AND I ARGUE, I feel as if God has abandoned me. Is this because I worship Norma instead of God? I want *her* love, *her* reassurances. I want to find safety in *her* arms. I've always insisted on a flesh-and-blood woman to worship, inspiration close at hand. What if God were even closer than that, closer than Norma's body pressed against me, closer than my own bones?

I CAN PRETEND that adoring Norma is the same as loving her — until she does something that isn't so adorable. Then I'm reminded it's an illusion I adore. Do I adore the illusion more than I love Norma?

THE BASIC ILLUSION is that we're separate — that there *is* a Norma, that there *is* a Sy. But, to quote former president Bill Clinton, "it depends upon what the meaning of the word *is* is."

SO SHE WAS GONE for an evening. And all those other evenings, the ones we spent together: aren't they gone, too? I can't claim them for my own. I can't claim Norma for my own. That's just one more illusion, the tenacious fantasy of a tenacious ego.

IF WE WERE IN BED, I'd want to make love. If we were talking, I'd want her undivided attention. Am I ever satisfied? What if she were ill? I'd be thankful she was breathing. I'd be thankful for her *life*.

IS NORMA MY TRUE LOVE? Only if I love her truly.

His Famous Melancholia

I CONTINUE TO BE AMAZED at all the bad habits I've picked up, as if I brought home another man's suitcase by mistake. The oddly tailored suits. The garish ties. And that hat! What sort of man would wear a ridiculous hat like that? I try it on, and I'm surprised: it fits perfectly. I stand in front of the mirror, give the brim a twist. I turn to the left, turn to the right. Not bad!

AM I READY TO SURRENDER — or do I need to crunch the numbers again? Just what is it about this world of illusion I still need to understand? The writer Satish Kumar tells of a man being chased by a wild elephant. The man climbs a tree and gets hold of a branch, but the elephant grabs the tree with his trunk and starts to shake it. Then, suddenly, the man is attacked by bees from a hive just above his head. But even as he's being stung, a few drops of honey trickle into his mouth, and the honey is deliciously sweet. He's savoring the taste when an angel flies by. The angel asks the man if he wants to be rescued. "Yes," the man says, "but can you wait until I get this next drop of honey? It's coming. See it coming? Just wait. . . ." The angel flies away. The man shouts after the angel, "But it's coming! Wait! I'll go with you after this drop!"

DO I REALLY NEED to understand myself better? Isn't that just another kind of accomplishment, another goal that's always out of reach? In therapy, I discover hidden stairwells, rooms within rooms. This is the sort of mansion a man could spend his whole life exploring, following clue after clue. But loving myself has nothing to do with following clues. Loving myself has nothing to do with understanding my story — such a beautiful story, such a poignant story. Just a story.

NOT MUCH HAPPENED yesterday. The sun set in the west after rising in the east. Job took it on the chin, as always. Narcissus, absorbed in his reflection, didn't move an inch.

IN THE MIDDLE OF THE NIGHT they came for me. They questioned me at length about where I'd come from and where I was going and whether I'd managed to make peace with myself. Had I learned to sit quietly for a minute or two? Was I able to serve others with no need to be praised? Was the Mystery mysterious enough for me?

NO MORE ROUGH STUFF, not this morning. I don't think the prisoner has anything left to say. After all, how many times can a man his age be bludgeoned with the same old existential truths? "Emptiness is form; form, emptiness." *Big deal*, he sighs. "Death comes suddenly and without warning." *Eat me.* Maybe there are more clues buried in his unhappy childhood. Maybe we need to get out the photo albums again, and the report cards, and the depositions from his boyhood friends. Still, if I have to study one more transcript or listen to one more bugged therapy session or connect one more set of dots to discern the underlying pattern of his famous melancholia, I'll scream. Is it possible he's simply of no use to us anymore? Should we take pity on the poor son of a bitch and let him go? That's assuming, of course, that he'd leave willingly and not insist that he's gotten used to being here, that it's the only home he knows.

ONCE A MAN IS FREE of illusion, the Buddha said, once he has freed himself from dwelling on sorrow, he will delight in existence and help reveal the path to many. Still, to free myself from dwelling on sorrow is no small task. In this culture of forced cheerfulness, it sometimes seems as if the grief I've repressed is the deepest truth of all. But just because something is buried doesn't mean it's the treasure I seek.

Magic Spells

NEARLY EVERY WEEKEND for the last six months, Norma
has been working for the Obama campaign: registering
new voters, going door to door to get out the vote, intoning
magic spells to make sure the giant lever in the basement
of Republican headquarters jams this year. And thanks
to her and millions of other Obama volunteers, yesterday
we witnessed a political miracle, heaven touching earth, a
last-minute pardon for a condemned prisoner. I can't recall
another time when I've felt so caught up in a moment of
collective celebration. I remember plenty of expressions of
angry protest, or collective grief, or numbed helplessness,
but not this sustained note of joy, this incredulity at our
great good fortune, sweeping up black and white, young
and old, women and men, Democrats and even some
Republicans. It's as if the U.S. has won the lottery. (What
were the odds?) It's as if our jumbo jet has touched down
safely after having circled the airport for hours, the fuel
gauge on empty, the pilot a rookie who'd never had to land
in a hurricane before.

Soon enough the campaign strategy will be dissected,
the miracle deconstructed, the butterfly pinned to the page.
Soon enough we'll be reminded that, despite the changes
President-elect Obama will bring, Mr. Money will still demand a seat at the head of the table. Frauds in high places
will still pose as patriots. Screwing up a job, a marriage,
or a planet will still be distressingly easy for the 59 million
Americans who voted for McCain, and the 68 million who

voted for Obama, and the 73 million eligible voters who cast no votes at all. For, as Eckhart Tolle writes, "If the structures of the human mind remain unchanged, we will always end up re-creating fundamentally the same world, the same evils, the same dysfunction."

But this morning, at least, you won't hear a peep out of me about the dying forests or the disappearing bees. This morning I'm celebrating the news that Democracy hasn't been imprisoned in some secure, undisclosed location but is confidently walking down the street. She's slapping people's backs and shaking their hands. She's wiping a tear from her cheek.

After the Next Deadline

I PROMISE NORMA I'm going to stop working so hard —
after the next deadline. At the moment I say it, I'm as ear-
nest as any religious fanatic convinced of his own ravings.
But if I died today, I'd be too busy to attend my own funeral:
there's the next issue to get out, the next meeting to attend,
the next stack of manuscripts to read. Maybe then I'd jump
in my car and try to get to the memorial service before it
was too late. I'd pay my respects to the man who worked
right up until the end, trying to save himself, or the world,
even after he'd realized he couldn't save either.

WHEN MY DAUGHTER Mara calls me a workaholic, I tell her
there's a world of difference between being addicted to work
and being dedicated to a labor of love. But I have to admit
that even a labor of love exacts a price. It's family lore that,
after having stayed up all night to finish an issue, I took my
young daughters to an art museum. While they looked at
Italian paintings from the fifteenth century, I leaned against
a wall, closed my eyes, and fell asleep.

I CAN'T BLAME the deadlines, or the e-mail, or the ringing
phone. They're not the reason I forget to pause, to breathe
deeply, to remember who I am. I always have a choice: to
stay grounded or to let myself be seduced. Busyness wraps
her arms around my neck, tells me what a great guy I am,
asks if I'd mind helping her with a few things. Oh, that
perfume!

ARE BUSYNESS AND FERMENT necessarily bad? In the movie *The Third Man*, a character observes that thirty years of turmoil in Italy under the Borgias produced Michelangelo, Leonardo da Vinci, and the Renaissance, while five hundred years of peace in Switzerland produced the cuckoo clock.

YESTERDAY I PICKED UP a twenty-year-old issue of *The Sun*. According to the masthead, four people worked with me in the office. The magazine had fourteen thousand subscribers. Today *The Sun* has nearly seventy thousand subscribers. Eleven people work beside me, and seven more work from home. That's eighteen in all: two baseball teams. Two teams, one manager — and perhaps not much of a manager at that. But I've always been ambivalent about being a boss or seeing myself as a "leader." MBA students with their eyes on the corner office take courses in leadership. I gravitate to Plato's model: the best leader is someone who isn't interested in the job.

Twenty years ago, I spent more time talking with my colleagues than I do now. No one was out of the loop. Had someone suggested that one day we'd use something called "e-mail" to communicate with one another, I'd have laughed. There were no formal job descriptions; we just had work to do, and we did it. Did people sometimes feel dissatisfied or unappreciated? Of course. It wasn't some golden age, but it was a different age. For me, personally, was it more agreeable? That's hard to say. Back then, I reminisced about the 1970s, when *The Sun* had fewer than a thousand subscribers and a staff of part-time volunteers.

I DIDN'T START *THE SUN* with a recipe. I made it up as I went along. I'm still making it up, even though the kitchen is so much bigger and better equipped now, with decent knives and sturdy pots and pans. But water still boils at the same temperature, and hunger is still hunger. I mean the hunger to break bread, and the other hunger: to break bread *together*.

I DREAMT THAT I WAS wandering around *The Sun's* office, only the furniture was different and the staff was different and no one knew who I was. Maybe I'm anticipating my next career move, when I segue from being *The Sun's* editor and publisher to *The Sun's* resident ghost, bewildered as only ghosts can be that everything has changed; not realizing — at least at first — that there are better ways to communicate with the still-living than to harass them with the usual ghost shtick. I told them I didn't want to be any trouble, but was there a chance they could set me up with an old manual typewriter and a desk made from a dead tree? They were all so young. They were all so busy. They had a deadline to meet, they said. I knew all about deadlines but had the good sense to keep my mouth shut. I was glad that they were working so hard. I was glad that they were publishing a real, honest-to-God independent magazine, even though *I* wasn't real anymore.

Ties! In 2009!

THE FIRST DECADE of the twenty-first century is nearly
over. If I'd read that sentence fifty years ago, I would have
imagined atomic-powered flying cars and world government, not traffic jams and global warming and people who
still wear dresses and high heels — high heels! — and
suits and ties. Ties! In 2009!

WE DEMAND THAT society change, ignoring how we
change individually: with the greatest effort, when there's
no other choice. We change through a lifetime of religious
devotion, or years of psychotherapy, or the grinding
lessons of raising a family, or a bad marriage or two. It's
tempting to imagine change comes easier — through a
weekend workshop, a new piece of legislation, a presidential election.

IN *A DIALOGUE ON LOVE*, Eve Kosofsky Sedgwick writes
about going into therapy for depression after having been
treated for cancer. She comes to see that her quickness
of mind was actually holding back her progress, because
she expected emotional change to be as easy to master
as a new literary theory. "It's hard to recognize that your
whole being, your soul, doesn't move at the speed of your
cognition . . . that it could take you a year to really know
something that you intellectually believe in a second." She
learned not to feel ashamed of this.

IF I DO NOTHING ELSE today, let me remember to stop maligning myself. What an ingrained habit that is: the finger-wagging and finger-pointing, my own Republican attack machine finding fault with nearly everything I do. What do I say to the bullies in the room, to the disembodied scolding voices of the dead parents and dead teachers and dead rabbis? They're all gone now, and I'm a man in my sixties, a voice of authority myself. Why be pushed around by ghosts? Why try to curry favor with them by making jokes at my own expense? What a rich tradition of self-effacing mockery I can draw upon: the gallows humor of *shtetl* Jews who considered it a good day if they could make their tormentors laugh. But those tormentors are dead, too, just more ghosts jockeying for a place in line. So listen up, ghosts: After all these years of being criticized and diminished and demeaned, I say, *Enough!* A man's home can't be his castle if he's living in a haunted house.

AS I WALKED ALONG a crowded street yesterday, something I'd read that morning by the Dalai Lama came to mind: "All living beings want happiness and not suffering." And, for a moment, I stopped noticing how different everyone looked. Behind our astonishing differences was something even more astonishing: our shared yearning to be happy and not to suffer. It didn't matter whether we were consciously aware of this. It didn't matter that we usually delude ourselves about the source of true happiness and look for it in all the wrong places. What mattered was that every single one of us wanted the same thing.

I'M LESS LIKELY TO JUDGE another person when I recall that I'm always working with insufficient information. Just as every tree has roots that are out of sight, underground, so does every person have roots the eye can't see. It's important for me to remember that this is equally true about me.

HOW LONG DOES IT TAKE to become enlightened? There's a Buddhist parable about a bird with a silk scarf in its beak. Once every hundred years, the bird flies over a mile-high mountain; each time, the scarf brushes the peak. How long does it take before the mountain is worn away? It won't do any good to rail at the bird for not flying faster. For not flying with a stick of dynamite in its beak.

The Meaning of Drowning

WHAT A COUPLE OF LOVEBIRDS Norma and I are these
days, relishing this season of relative tranquillity. At this
age we can't fool ourselves into thinking it will go on forever — the tranquillity, that is; the love, I can't say. At the
door to that mystery, stronger men than I sit weeping.

THAT NORMA AND I STILL DELIGHT in each other's company is a miracle I foolishly take for granted. But I know
it's a miracle because I know I'm a mess: fiercely possessive,
hopelessly dependent. Let's face it, decades of "working
on myself" haven't gotten me very far. I'm like a guy with
a rusty car that's been on blocks for longer than anyone
can remember, yet whose engine he still imagines he can
rebuild — if only he had the right parts; if only he had
the right tools; if only he had a user's manual written in a
language he could understand.

LAST NIGHT, A MINOR DISAGREEMENT between Norma
and me turned into the worst kind of conflagration: an
argument about how we argue. This morning, the last thing
I feel like doing is finding the perfect place to celebrate our
anniversary. But I promised I'd take care of it. Maybe a
stateroom on the *Titanic*? If we're lucky, we'll end up in the
same lifeboat together. Or maybe we'll go down with the
ship, arguing about the meaning of drowning.

ALL THAT TALK ABOUT *differences*, but at 2 AM we both woke up, needing to pee.

ECKHART TOLLE: "If her past were your past, her pain your pain, her level of consciousness your level of consciousness, you would think and act exactly as she does. With this realization comes forgiveness, compassion, peace."

THERE'S NO BLAME. It's hard to say that. No blame. (Say it again.)

NORMA DOESN'T MIND when I write about our marriage, even if I mention her snoring, or an argument we've had, or the ridiculously large bed she still insists we sleep in, which should have come with a global-positioning system so I can find her in the middle of the night. No matter what I write, she says, she's "narcissistic enough" to enjoy it. I ask if I can quote her. "What do you think?" she replies.

The Lie I Tell Myself

SO LITTLE PROGRESS to report: Osama bin Laden hasn't been captured, nor have I ferreted out the terrorists in my own psyche. Loneliness seems to have a life of its own. So do lust and greed and fear.

EVEN ON THIS SUNNY DAY, a dark cloud. Even though my wife loves me, and my daughters are healthy, and Barack Obama is president. The Prozac helped again; it really did. I was happier, less anxious, more productive. But after a while I missed my old self: his intact libido, his salty tears, even some of his convoluted fears. Now he's back, and I wonder how far away my Happiness is today. Even on foot, she can cover quite a distance, sauntering down a country road or winking at a driver and hitching a ride. Maybe she asked to be dropped off at the airport, where she cashed in her frequent-smiler miles and, at this very moment, is relaxing in first class, the distance between us growing vaster by the minute, as my Happiness flies away from me, sipping champagne and eating hot nuts.

I FILLED THE WORLD with my lament, but the world had broken better men than me. My sins were of the lesser variety: I ate too much and talked too much and played too much with my golden zipper. I didn't stay in touch with old friends. I didn't pray every day for the poor. The world was used to this and signed off on my paperwork with a distracted air, too busy even to notice my confession.

THE LIE I TELL MYSELF is that I'm not good enough. By whose standards? By standards that are impossible to attain — certainly impossible for me to attain. I never was a straight-A student, and I'm not a straight-A student now. I make mistakes. I don't always live up to my potential. My sexual imagination is X-rated, not politically correct, sometimes not even anatomically correct. The lie I tell myself is that God is appalled.

MUST IT BE LIKE THIS? I ask the mirror. *Don't ask me*, the mirror says.

IS IT POSSIBLE to live each day knowing that everything will go wrong — that everything is falling apart right now — yet remembering, too, that this in no way denies the love at the heart of existence?

THE SUFIS SAY that anything you can lose in a shipwreck isn't yours.

I THOUGHT I WAS DROWNING, so I raised my arms and cried out to a God I didn't believe in. And my heart, foolish heart, opened like a great white sail. And the God I didn't believe in was the sea. And the God I didn't believe in was the wind.

WHAT CAN I BE GRATEFUL FOR this morning? I'm grateful for my trillions of cells chattering away in a language I'll never comprehend. I'm grateful that I couldn't run all the way up the hill today; thank God for hills. I'm grateful that, while reading *The New York Times*, I could get only halfway up the hill of understanding; thank God for human nature. I'm grateful for the end of eight murderously long years of George W. Bush's presidency, setting his black mark on the first decade of the twenty-first century. I'm grateful that no city has been wiped out by a nuclear weapon in sixty-four years. I'm grateful that more Americans believe in democracy than you could guess from reading the headlines.

Her Secret Police

I LEAVE TOWN tomorrow to attend a conference for writers and the rest of the kitchen help: editors and publishers and agents and writing teachers and literary scholars and literary hangers-on. I rarely attend such events, preferring to remain in the kitchen and continue chopping vegetables: my small contribution to keeping the hungry fed. It will be gratifying, I'm sure, to talk with other chefs about the kind of knives we use, and the angle at which we hold them, and how brave we were the last time we nicked our fingers. And the recipes we share will be mouthwatering. And, being only human, we'll forget that the menu isn't the meal.

I COULDN'T SLEEP LAST NIGHT. Too much thunder and lightning. Norma loves thunderstorms, but I'm unable to sleep through them. I feel as if I'm being disrespectful to an angry Father: God pounding his fist on the table, the original shock and awe.

So I got up and read manuscripts for a while, and struggled with whether to accept any of them for publication, and probably stirred up some bad dreams for writers who'd hoped for a different outcome. Since *The Sun* receives nearly a thousand submissions a month, I've had to learn numerous ways to say no, the way the Inuit have so many words for snow. I try to be kind, but there's no denying the blast of Arctic air a writer must feel when she finds another rejection note in the mail. Maybe she's used to this kind of weather by now, or maybe her mouth tightens and her eyes well up.

I started *The Sun* in order to relieve, not create, suffering. But it's impossible to publish the magazine without letting down thousands of writers year after year. Then again, I remind myself, every *yes* in our lives arises from the rubble of innumerable *no*s: we move to this town, not that town; bring home the brown puppy from the pound, not the black one. Even the soldier surrounded by enemies raises his rifle and takes aim at just one. Finally I turned off the lamp and tried to get back to sleep, wondering whether a writer somewhere was dreaming of white envelopes falling from a winter sky. Which one will she open first? That, she thinks, is what she hates the most: having to decide.

THE WOMAN ASKED ME what kind of writers I'm looking for. I don't remember what I told her. This is what I wish I'd said: I'm looking for a writer who doesn't know where the sentence is leading her; a writer who starts with her obsessions and whose heart is bursting with love; a writer sly enough to give the slip to her secret police, the ones who know her so well, the ones with the power to accuse and condemn in the blink of an eye. It's all right that she doesn't know what she's thinking until she writes it, as if the words already existed somewhere and drew her to them. She may not know how she got there, but she knows when she's arrived.

NO MATTER HOW MANY hours I put in, I never get caught up, never take a step into the promised land rumored to lie beyond these stacks of unread manuscripts and unanswered mail. I promise myself I'll work harder, but *The Sun*'s readership keeps growing, and so does the staff, and I'm busier than ever. To stay faithful to why I'm publishing *The Sun*, I need to remember the difference between what's genuinely important and what merely clamors for my attention. As the journalist Murray Kempton once wrote: "The devil never comes offering you something evil. The devil comes offering you a larger audience."

COURAGE FAILS ME. I want the easy way out: a long morning in bed with no decisions to make except how long to kiss Norma; no writers to disappoint; no readers to grumble that my forlorn expression will drive the country into a major depression. I don't want to be there when the indictment is handed down, just like yesterday and the day before. Guilty as charged, Your Honor. Yes, I'm working too hard. Yes, I'm not working hard enough.

Teacher of the Year

WE'RE ALL CROWDED into the hospital corridor, waiting
for word about the ailing economy. No, it doesn't look
good: vital signs worse each day, internal bleeding, liver
and kidney functions starting to shut down. *Do you remember*,
someone whispers, *when she started partying all night
with those subprime lenders, then began gulping down credit-swap
derivatives as if they were vitamins?* Of course the hospital staff
has seen it all before. The U.S. economy seems addicted to
these periodic cycles of boom and bust. Let's face it: collectively we're like some hopeless romantic who moves from
one affair to another (the junk-bond bubble, the dot-com
bubble, the mortgage-backed-securities bubble), always in
love at the beginning — what's not to love? — and always
in despair at the end. Eventually we rise from the ashes,
sweep them under the rug, vow never to make the same
mistake again — and, after a suitable period of mourning,
fling open the windows and start flirting with the new
neighbor, who looks like a million bucks.

WE ATE TOO MUCH. Of course we did. It was a Thanks-
giving feast, here in the land of plenty. Go ahead, America,
take another bite. The most powerful nation in the world
doesn't have to apologize for being a little hungry.

MY DESK IS A MESS. My heart is a mess. Human history
is a mess. The global financial system? Let's see: one word,
rhymes with *guess*. Politics? Don't make me laugh, don't

make me cry, don't make me spontaneously combust as
I read the headlines. Even with Barack Obama in the
White House, the United States is a mess. Washington,
D.C.? Clean up your room! Moscow, London, Beijing?
Sweep the floor! Organize your sock drawer!

YES, WE'RE IN A RECESSION. But sooner or later each of
us will lose something more important than our savings
or our job. Will we have the resilience to deal with sudden
illness or injury or any of the misfortunes life may have in
store? I've learned that every experience can be a teaching
— if I'm willing to see it that way. Suffering, too, can be
a teaching. In fact, suffering gets the teacher-of-the-year
award because I always sit up and pay attention when
I'm in physical pain or when my heart has been broken or
when I witness the anguish of someone I love. To honor
the teaching doesn't mean welcoming suffering with open
arms, or looking for the silver lining of a tragedy with
the kind of relentless optimism that denies painful feelings. Blessings in disguise remain disguised until they're
good and ready to reveal themselves — and even then, the
blessing might simply be that a particular setback has
taught me to live more fully in the present, or deepened my
compassion for others going through a similar difficulty, or
underscored the paradox that we're ultimately alone and
inextricably bound to one another.

Many Alarm Clocks

I DREAMT THAT a beautiful stranger had fallen in love with me. The only way to find out where she lived, however, was to look her up on Facebook, which I'd steadfastly refused to join. So that's what I get for my neo-Luddite posturing, for having told a friend yesterday that the world needs an About-Facebook.

WHO I AM IS WHO I AM, whether I confuse myself with a saint one minute or a sinner the next; whether I'm rigorously faithful to my wife by day or a serial adulterer in my dreams; whether my charitable donations are deemed sufficient by a well-fed jury of my peers or judged a capital offense by the hungry mob at the door.

RAM DASS SAYS that when you're walking down the street and you're hungry, all you see are restaurants. When you're horny, all you see are attractive strangers. When you're looking for God, all you see is God.

I PAY TOO MUCH ATTENTION to what I'm thinking and feeling, not enough attention to who I really am. My busy mind loves to keep busy, just as a child loves to play. There's nothing wrong with being a child, but there comes a time to put away childish things. I love the games I played as a child. I love what they taught me. But would I now choose to devote all day to playing Monopoly or Scrabble or Prince Valiant? Instead I spend all day playing

Sy Safransky. I've learned most of the rules; I'm an experienced player. It's so tempting to set up the pieces again and again.

BEFORE FALLING ASLEEP last night, I read the words of a spiritual master who said his aim was to pry me loose from my illusory "me-ness" and awaken me — right here, right now — to my true nature. Enlightenment isn't for just a chosen few, he insisted, nor is it necessary to meditate for thirty years before seeing through the illusion of separateness. His words stirred something in me, since, as a young man, I'd imagined I would become enlightened by the time I was old. But now that I'm an old man, becoming enlightened in this lifetime seems as plausible as recapturing my lost youth. This makes the notion of a sudden awakening very appealing. But so are advertisements for skin creams that promise to erase wrinkles or a little blue pill that will let me go on pretending I'm the greatest lover in the world.

I WANTED TO SLEEP. Of course I did. I wanted to stay lost in illusion. But somewhere down the hall an alarm kept ringing.

G.I. GURDJIEFF: "A man may be awakened by an alarm clock. But the trouble is that a man gets accustomed to the clock far too quickly and ceases to hear it. Many alarm clocks are necessary and always new ones."

TO WANT NOTHING BUT GOD — what would that be like? Getting on an airplane, nervous about flying, what would it be like to want only God? On the longest, dreariest night of the year, when I'm melancholy and restless, what would it be like to want only God? What would it be like to give up the foolish dream that living a more spiritual life is going to save me, like a wise investment in the stock market; to see it all come crashing, and still want only God?

Back to the Garden

AS INDEPENDENCE DAY approaches, I wonder what we're supposed to give a country on its 234th birthday. Solar panels on every roof? Extraordinary teachers in every school? An equitable tax system that demands more from the rich? How about a magic wand that turns slow trains into fast trains, and fast-food restaurants into slow-food restaurants, and all the charlatans in Congress into dedicated public servants? And while we're at it, how about tearing down that wall in our collective psyche that separates the present from the past? More than 15 million indigenous people occupied North America before Europeans arrived in the New World (new to the Europeans, at least). By 1910 — because of disease and war and forced migration — their numbers had been reduced to fewer than half a million. And today they're largely forgotten except as a plot device in Hollywood westerns. We celebrate the birth of our nation on the Fourth of July. On what day do we mourn those who died because of our ancestors' imperial ambitions?

CAN I GO A WHOLE DAY without complaining about the CEOs raping the planet? Without complaining about the feckless politicians cheering them on? Without complaining about the United States becoming a wholly owned subsidiary of the highest bidder? Without complaining about this world of sorrows as I slip another bright idea into God's suggestion box?

NORMA KEEPS REMINDING ME I can't predict the future. But here I am, exactly as old as I imagined I'd be this fall. What else did I get right? That the earth still orbits the sun; that a light-year is still a light-year; that I drag some darkness with me wherever I go. At night, under stars that blaze in and out of existence, shall I complain that the days are too short and the nights too long? What a crybaby I've become, wanting Mother Nature to tuck me in at the end of the day and read me a happy story — no floods, no earthquakes, no sidewalks too hot to touch.

I WONDER WHETHER we'll soon have just two seasons: Hot and Very Hot. Or Hot, Very Hot, and You've Got to Be Kidding. Still, didn't I vow to stop gnashing my teeth about global warming? If I knew this was my last day on earth, would I spend time condemning my brothers and sisters for the mistakes we've made, or deriding myself for being just another greedy American who uses a disproportionate share of the world's resources? Maybe there was once a golden age in which humans lived in energy-efficient harmony, women doing half the hunting and men half the gathering, the sex always sacred, no carbon footprint because we flew only in our dreams. But I have no idea how to get back to the Garden.

So I just want to say: Forgive us for letting the Industrial Revolution get out of hand. Forgive us for swapping the wooden hoe for the horse-drawn plow, then trading in the horse for an air-conditioned tractor. Forgive me for driving to work instead of bicycling — in an old Volvo instead of a hybrid — and for being less concerned with nature than with human nature.

HOW HARD IT IS to change the simplest habit. No wonder, then, that society's bad habits can seem so intractable. Yet whenever I'm finally able to open a stuck window in my psyche, my notion of what's possible is profoundly altered, and society begins to seem less monolithic. We really do teach by example, and it's impossible to say what the effect of even the smallest change might be.

Animal Behavior

NOW THAT BARACK OBAMA is president, the cats still need
to be fed. The weeds still need to be pulled. Each day still
has only twenty-four hours. Each life still has only so many
years. Everyone everywhere will still end six feet under,
loved ones not even a president can save.

Now that Barack Obama is president, Catholics still go
to confession. Muslims still pray five times a day. Orthodox
Jews must still obey 613 commandments, including one that
prohibits any additional commandments.

Now that Barack Obama is president, suffering still
resists all attempts to explain it. We still need to feed the
hungry, shelter the homeless, and comfort the afflicted.
People everywhere will continue to endure hurricanes and
tornadoes and heat waves and earthquakes and floods and
blizzards. Three things in life are still important, as Henry
James said: "The first is to be kind. The second is to be kind.
And the third is to be kind."

Now that Barack Obama is president, Americans are still
only 5 percent of the world's population. Earth is still only
one of eight planets — poor defrocked Pluto! — circling the
sun. The sun is still only one of more than 100 billion stars
in the Milky Way galaxy. The Milky Way is still only one of
more than 100 billion galaxies in the visible universe, most of
them containing billions upon billions of stars.

Now that Barack Obama is president, the realm of the
invisible remains invisible. Nature's laws remain unchanged.
All night the dream factories still run at full capacity.

MY CAT FRANNY is meowing; she wants another treat. Don't we all. Republicans want to regain a majority in Congress this fall and take back the White House in 2012. What a treat that would be for the wealthiest 1 percent of Americans. With everything they have, so many of them are meowing for more: now, how rich is that? Of course, there's nothing wrong with Franny wanting more. She's not being sinful; it's animal behavior. Are the wealthiest Americans just a bunch of animals? Yes — and so are the rest of us: rich and poor, black and white, men with heavy beards and women with angelic complexions, Republican animals, Democratic animals, Christian and Jewish and Muslim animals. Imagine how much meowing God has to listen to.

IT'S FOGGY THIS MORNING, but I won't blame the Weather Channel. I stayed up too late last night, but I won't blame the Internet or the computer that sits on my lap like a household pet who responds to my every command. Barack Obama hasn't kept all his promises, but I won't blame him for having a hard time governing the same country that elected Nixon and Reagan and Bush the elder and Bush the prodigal son. The casualty figures in Afghanistan keep rising, but I won't blame the United States or the Taliban for making war, not love — for hasn't this been the habitual behavior of humans for as long as other humans have been condemning it?

Tomorrow Never Comes

MORE WINE! I tell the waiter. More bread! It's my birthday. I want this lovely evening to last. No problem, he says. Keep eating and drinking like there's no tomorrow. But do I mind if he clears a few dishes? Do I mind if he starts sweeping the floor?

TOMORROW NEVER COMES. But death comes. Wake up!

I'M LOOKING FOR MY BODY. The last time I saw it was weeks ago at the gym. My body doesn't call. My body doesn't write. *You're taking me for granted*, my body might have said before it stopped wasting its breath; I can't be sure because I was listening to the radio. I was driving to work. *What about biking to work?* my body might have whispered. But I was listening to my messages. I was surfing the Internet.

IS THERE ANYONE who complains about me more than I complain about myself? I could fill *The Sun*'s Correspondence section with one letter after another, the handwriting on them all the same: Maybe you've written everything of value you're ever going to write, Mr. Safransky. Maybe you're an old dog who'd rather lick himself than learn new tricks. Maybe it's time to say goodbye, Mr. Safransky. We know you're having a hard time hiking up this winding road. No one really cares if you take off your pack, lie down, and catch up on all the sleep you've missed. No one really cares if you've left the best part of yourself in the twentieth century, Mr. Safransky — or, frankly, which part of you that is.

YESTERDAY IS GONE. "Wednesday," we called it. So far, Thursday is looking a lot like Wednesday except for one obvious difference: Wednesday is no more. Wednesday has ceased to be. Yes, Wednesday is like the dead parrot in that Monty Python skit: Stiff. Bereft of life. Just as the parrot is an ex-parrot, Wednesday is an ex-Wednesday. And if it happened to Wednesday, can't it happen to Thursday? Why study Buddhist texts on impermanence when I can just sit here and watch Thursday slip away?

NO COMPLAINING that we weren't consulted when they wrote the laws of impermanence. No complaining that actual mileage varies from decade to decade, no matter how many vitamins we take. No complaining that death comes for us all, even if we never hurt a fly; even if we follow the commandments; even if we run five miles, not three miles, score the winning touchdown, single-handedly save the world. No complaining that death is unimpressed.

I WANTED TO MILK THE DAY for all it was worth, as if Time were a cow and all I needed was a bucket. But no sooner did I get started than Time swished her tail and the bright new day was gone. *How could that be?* I gasped. Time raised her head and looked at me with eyes so big you'd think there would be room in them for some compassion. *Don't forget your bucket,* Time said.

IT'S A COLD WINTER MORNING, still dark outside, and I'm hurtling through space at thousands of miles an hour with a cup of hot coffee in my hand. Amazing! Because I've been in this body for nearly sixty-five of Earth's orbits around the sun, I'll soon have enough frequent-flyer miles to qualify for Medicare. Eventually I'll have enough points to request a corner suite in a nursing home, where a pretty aide will coo sweet nothings while giving me a sponge bath. Amazing! And then come the drugs: ketamine, lorazepam, and enough high-grade medical marijuana to impress even an old pothead like me — not to mention my own morphine drip. Now, how amazing is that!

Too Hot to Touch

I'M STILL NOT USED TO writing "2010," even though the year is more than half over. I'm still not used to living on a planet that's too hot to touch. I'm still not used to qualifying for the senior discount at the health-food store. I'm still not used to Barack Obama being a man, not a god.

MY CAT NIMBUS is sick. Our veterinarian, who makes house calls, will arrive soon in his twenty-four-foot-long animal hospital on wheels. I wonder how many miles to the gallon it gets. But with my cat's well-being at stake, do I really care? Recently I've been shopping for a car: maybe a new car, maybe a used car, maybe an abandoned car I can drive when I'm feeling abandoned. I'll probably buy an environmentally friendly hybrid. Still, when it comes to those I love, be they cats or humans, what price am I willing to ask my good friend the earth to pay?

I CAN'T SEEM TO get it right. I don't give enough to the poor, or remember to be thankful for every bite, or fully grasp what a marvelous world we're destroying. Everything that should matter all the time matters only some of the time; everything that should never matter — well, sometimes it matters quite a bit.

I'M SURPRISED THAT SOMEONE as notoriously impatient as I am isn't more critical of President Obama. Maybe it's because I know how challenging it can be to run even a small nonprofit organization like *The Sun*, or to reform my own healthcare system: to remember to exercise every day and take my vitamins and get enough sleep. And let's not even talk about my mental health: my worries piling up faster than the national debt; those fears I've dragged from decade to decade, as much a part of me by now as some huge military budget I'm unable to whittle down. In any event, I'm still willing to give Obama the benefit of the doubt. Of course he's the consummate politician; how else could he have been elected president? Of course during his first year in office he hasn't righted every social wrong. How many wrongs did I right last year?

BEFORE THE MIDTERM elections roll around, let me be clear: I'm not a candidate. Not for most devoted editor. Not for most devoted husband. Not for God's most devoted servant, down on my knees before the altar of truth, waxing the floor until it shines. I'm not promising to feed the hungry instead of reaching for a second helping. I'm not promising to open a nationwide chain of soup kitchens with linen tablecloths and a maître d' who seats only the poorest of the poor. If nominated, I will not accept. If elected, I will not serve. If forced to take the oath, I will not promise to be the change you can believe in. If I do make such a promise, I promise not to keep it.

I SAY GOOD MORNING to the homeless man, then feel embarrassed, as if cheerfulness were a luxury.

ADMITTEDLY HUMANS aren't doing so well. But put any other mammal behind the wheel of a shiny new Cadillac, 440 horses under the hood, and see if it does any better. Would a chimpanzee willingly relinquish the keys after sitting through a PowerPoint presentation on climate change by Al Gore? So let's show a little compassion for our not-so-evolved species. I mean, how many millennia did it take Homo sapiens to harness fire, or plant crops, or invent the wheel? The Industrial Revolution didn't begin until the eighteenth century; is it any surprise that it's taking us a while to clean up the mess? How long does it take any of us to learn from our bad decisions and failed relationships and lousy habits we can't seem to break? Yes, the planet is getting hotter. But even if we were crowded together on a slow boat to hell, wouldn't we want to extend some mercy to our fellow passengers?

JUST GIVE ME the good news this morning, and let me hear it sung! I want glorious cantatas. I want soaring arias. I want the music of the spheres ringing in my ears. Single-Payer Healthcare Reform Signed Into Law! Scientists Discover Another World Hidden Within This World! Man Loses Virginity With Woman He Adores!

The Old Jail Keeper

WHEN ASKED HOW sexual passion changes with age, Sophocles said, "I feel as if I had escaped from a mad and furious master." In my mid-sixties, I know what he means, but there are plenty of nights when I miss the old jail keeper and wouldn't mind being locked up again — maybe in the cell where Norma and I used to make love from dusk to dawn; or where we made love a few times a day, not a few times a week. Still, I try not to take it personally that I've lived this long. So I kiss Norma's neck and brush a lock of hair from her face. I kiss her eyes. My hands have been everywhere, and they go there again. And I praise the fire that burns in winter, and the heat that rises, and the plume of sparks. And I praise the gods of the marriage bed, the cat that still meows, the dog that still barks.

NORMA AND I HAVE BEEN together nearly thirty years, and I'm still the hopelessly romantic schmuck I was when we met. While she was away last week, how did I feel? Like a question without an answer. Like a column of figures that didn't add up. And when she returned? As happy as a thief slipping into a rich man's house at night. As happy as Winter opening his eyes one morning and seeing the face of Spring.

NORMA SAYS THAT when I take a shower in the morning, she lies in bed, half asleep, pretending it's raining. She loves the rain. I read that W.C. Fields loved the rain, too, because it conveyed to him a sense of humankind's insignificance.

He would leave his house during a sudden downpour and stand in the rain, bareheaded and serene.

I WAKE UP in a familiar body on a familiar planet. It's still dark outside. I have every confidence, however, that the sun will soon light up the sky. How do I know this? Call me a man of faith. I believe in this spinning planet. I believe in the tides and in the seasons and in the crickets who are chirping this morning. I believe, because I just looked it up, that the chirping sound is made by male crickets rubbing their forewings together — serenading the females, I suppose. I believe in courtship. I believe in love's redemptive power. I believe that the first sound my wife will hear this morning will be me whispering her name. I believe in each and every letter that spells "Norma." I like to curl up inside the O as if it were home.

ÉMILE DE GIRARDIN: "A woman whom we truly love is a religion."

AND THERE'S STILL NOTHING I'd rather do than wrap my arms around her and lose myself inside her, lose the tickets and the passport and my name and date of birth; lose the body I've never learned to love; lose the words I love too much.

I USED TO THINK I was a great lover. Now I understand: the greatness is in the love, not the man.

Gauzy Curtain

ANY DAY NOW, any hour, the phone will ring and I'll get
the news that I'm the grandfather of an infinitely wise
and beautifully proportioned baby girl, fully equipped to
wiggle her ten fingers and ten toes, to nurse at her mother's
breast, and, before she's twenty, to discover how to turn
daydreams into reality without the use of fossil fuels; and,
before she's thirty, to use moonlight to cure migraine head-
aches and broken hearts; and, before she's forty, to run for
president. Win or lose, honey, I'll love you just the same.

I'M NOT SOMEONE who thinks a lot about the future. Maybe that's because I'm grounded in the present; maybe it's
because I'm a man who lacks vision. But yesterday, when
I held my three-day-old granddaughter in my arms, time's
gauzy curtain parted for a moment: with good genes and a
touch of luck, I realized, this little girl may still be alive in
the year 2100. Until that moment, 2100 was an abstraction
to me, a page from the distant future. As I cradled Katharine, the future seemed closer.

KATHARINE WAS BORN in twenty-first-century Los Angeles, with its millions of people and billions of cars, its
beautiful people, its invisible people, its not-so-invisible
smog. She picked a moment when the earth is growing
warmer and the odds against humanity are growing
longer. Between now and 2100 she's likely to experience
breakthroughs in medical science and nanotechnology and

clean energy that are unimaginable today. But because of global climate change, she may also face an all-you-can't-eat buffet of droughts and heat waves and viral pandemics and mass migrations and wars over arable land. In 2100 will the protest signs read, NO BLOOD FOR WATER? Will the Far Right have invented a flag that flutters whether or not there's a breeze?

WHEN MY DAUGHTER MARA first placed Katharine in my arms, I felt some trepidation. The last time I'd held a newborn had been when Mara's sister, Sara, was born. *Saturday Night Fever* was playing in movie theaters, gas cost sixty-three cents a gallon, and Jimmy Carter was president. Katharine was half asleep, here and not here, a tender shoot still drenched in mystery; an utterly unselfconscious, exquisitely vulnerable being who wasn't afraid and wasn't ashamed and wasn't trying to impress anyone. Everyone who's seen her says she's beautiful, which is true. But to my mind most newborns look pretty much alike, with their puffy eyes and wrinkled skin and oddly shaped skulls, the inevitable consequence of being curled up for months in a narrow compartment, then pushed out the door when the swaying, lumbering train finally arrives at the station. So when we say a newborn is beautiful, maybe we're really describing how we feel in that infant's presence. When we're face to face with the unfathomable miracle of a human incarnation, our hearts open. What's more beautiful than that?

KATHARINE IS FOUR DAYS OLD. I'm nearly twenty-four thousand days old. I hope she'll pay attention when I try to give her some advice about our bewildering species; about all the rules and all the exceptions to the rules; about the reckless, savage side of human nature and the indestructible essence in each of us that aspires to something greater than fame or riches or worldly power. But I'm mindful that it's Mara and her husband Chris's turn now, not a second act for a bearded patriarch who knows as little about being a grandfather as he once did about being a father.

HOW AMAZING TO SEE the newborn I used to carry in my arms holding *her* newborn in *her* arms. What's it like for Mara to watch her father become a grandfather? When she sees me holding Katharine, does she, too, feel closer to the inexorable turning of the wheel?

KATHARINE CARRIES ONE-QUARTER of my genetic heritage. Which quarter? Who cares? Maybe I'm missing something, but I've never been concerned with how many of my genes are passed from one generation to the next, as if my DNA were an Olympic torch to be kept aloft as it's handed from runner to runner. Isn't Katharine's genetic heritage the same as that of the whole human race — not just my genes but *our* genes? Why cultivate an attachment to how much of me is wrapped around a tiny spiral helix? Why look for signs of "Sy" in "Katharine" as she grows up?

Will that make her even more special in my eyes? More worthy of my love?

WHAT IF WE EXTENDED as much kindness and generosity to everyone as we do to our own children and grandchildren? It's shameful that I still make a distinction between the small number of people who matter the most to me and the nearly 7 billion other humans on the planet. Then again, it's so much easier to love the infant in your arms than to embrace the moody co-worker, the eccentric neighbor, the politician who lets you down.

Six Different Kinds of Silence

WHEN I WENT RUNNING this morning, I thought to myself, *Not bad for a man my age.* Then, as clearly as if she were running beside me, a recently departed friend whispered: *Enough already. The body is just an address. Nice house. Lovely neighborhood. Congratulations. Just an address.*

MY NEIGHBOR NANCY, who is in her eighties, was making her way down the street with her walker. Not having talked with her since her stroke, I asked how she was. "Good," she said. She asked the same of me. I managed a noncommittal "OK." She asked what I was doing these days. "Oh, the usual," I replied. "Reading, writing, worrying." She laughed. "At my age," she said, "you don't worry anymore." "Well," I said, "that's something to look forward to."

THE YEAR IS NEARLY OVER, but I'm in no rush for it to end. I want to slow time down, not speed it up. I guess I'm hungry for the kind of long, slow morning no one has tasted since the dawn of the Industrial Revolution; a morning before computers, before television, before the rhythmic thumping of Johannes Gutenberg's printing press woke everyone in Europe; a morning filled with six different kinds of silence and slathered in sunlight so thick it made you dizzy just to open your eyes.

A TELEMARKETER CALLS with "important information" about a prepaid burial plan. I politely decline his offer.

Later, I ask Norma if she still intends to be cremated after she dies. She says she's not sure. "Why?" I ask. "I don't want to contribute to global warming," she says. This is an excellent example of how different we are: My thoughtful and compassionate wife, even when contemplating her own demise, is still concerned about the fate of the planet. I, on the other hand, don't want to be cremated because *I don't want to die*.

"WHAT COULD BE more wonderful," I asked Norma, "than not to be afraid of dying?" She asked if I knew the French phrase for *orgasm*. "Yes," I said, "*le petit mort* — the little death." She nodded, then replied, "Maybe dying is the great orgasm."

I WONDER: is reincarnation real or just some goofy idea I picked up in a former lifetime?

ONE OF OUR READERS told me this story: While driving to work one day, she heard her aunt Clara, who'd been dead for twenty-five years, tell her to hit the brakes. A moment later, a truck ran a stoplight and barreled through the intersection she'd been approaching. She pulled over to the side of the road, shaken and amazed. To her aunt, she said, "Talk to me." Her aunt replied, "I'm not here for your distraction."

THIS MORNING, I OPEN Walt Whitman's *Leaves of Grass* to this line: "And to die is different from what anyone supposed, and luckier."

I'M HERE AT THE INTERSECTION of flesh and spirit: a six-foot-tall biped with my feet on the ground and my head in the clouds; 165 pounds of muscle and fat and memories and opinions walking upright on an oxygen-rich planet. This morning I'm feeling particularly buoyant because I dreamt that beings from an advanced civilization gave me a mind-expanding drug. Well, their civilization was certainly advanced when it came to hallucinogens. Or maybe it had simply been too long since I'd had the blinders removed and glimpsed the radiant mystery at the heart of existence. I experienced oneness not as a mere abstraction but as an undeniable reality, as plain as the nose on God's face. I knew in my bones, in my cells, in the very atoms of "me" that everyone is part of the same living intelligence, as are the trees, the rocks, the sky; that separateness is an illusion; that death is nothing to fear. One look at my benevolent companions told me they knew it, too. It was hard to say whether they'd also taken the drug or had evolved this way after innumerable virtuous lifetimes. In my dream, it didn't matter; I'd woken up.

They Came for Their Lessons

HAPPY BIRTHDAY, DAD. How long has it been since I've
felt your hand on my shoulder? Maybe it's been there all
along, guiding me. Here, among the living, we speculate
endlessly about such things. Our pictures have all the
subtlety of a paint-by-numbers kit, but that's the best we
can do. Is there anything you want to tell me about the city
of the dead? Are you wiser now? Are you happier? Do you
still get together with your friends on Friday nights to play
pinochle, or did you leave all that behind, like your job,
your wife, your daughter, your son? I'll leave it all behind,
too, won't I? Everything that's so important to me now,
everything I can't imagine living without. Just as, once, I
couldn't imagine living without you.

I'M OUT OF TOWN with Norma, and I'm homesick. I miss
my cats. I miss my friends. But I know that once I'm back
home, I'll miss something I'm never able to put my finger
on. Is it something from the past? Growing up in Brooklyn?
My father's big hands, the smell of his cigars? My mother's
arms, her breast, her breath? Maybe I'm nostalgic for the
night they lay entwined, and half of me met the other half.

I FELT GLOOMY YESTERDAY and went for a walk. My
spirits were revived when I passed two elderly men having
a lively conversation. Just seeing them was comforting
and made me realize I spend too much time with people
younger than I am. I need the company of men old enough

to remind me that women were never the problem or the answer to the problem; that everything the holy books say is true really is true, but that life isn't a book. I thought of my father, dead so many years. I thought, *Even a grown man sometimes needs a hand on his shoulder.*

I SAID SOMETHING scornful about my mother, then felt sad that I'd soiled the air with my words, sad that I was still grousing about this woman who'd tried her best to be a loving mother. She wasn't perfect. Neither am I. She could be blind to the consequences of her actions. So can I. She wasn't better than me or worse than me. If blacks can forgive whites, if Jews can forgive Germans, surely I can forgive this woman whose life was harder than mine — a woman who, as a teenager, lost her mother to cancer and was deserted by her father; who had to drop out of high school during the Depression to go to work; who was sexually molested by an uncle who took her in. She never had the benefit of a college education or an understanding therapist. She built her own defenses, built them so high that I often couldn't see over them; so I built my own.

I COULDN'T LAY DOWN my weapons. Well, my sword, but not my shield.

IT'S HARD TO ACCEPT that my mother and I came together in this life to share something difficult; that our relationship wore us down the way a mighty river wears down a rock wall, eventually creating something of beauty and depth. Part of me still longs for a storybook mother, and another part knows that the more interesting story is the one we wrote: a story of love and loss, of two souls calling to each other from across the great divide of their seeming separateness.

SO HERE WE ARE, my long-dead son. Thirty-eight years have come and gone. For three days you struggled to stay alive. I buried your ashes. I looked for a sign. The years march on. Now I'm sixty-five. I still search for answers. I read between the lines. But the Mystery's the Mystery. We can laugh or we can cry. Sweet boy, you've been gone a long, long time.

I BOW TO THE ANCESTORS. They came for their lessons; I've come for mine.

All the News Will Be Recycled

IN THE CHURCH OF MORNING, I give thanks for a good cup of coffee, and for the chain of events that brings this coffee to my table. I'm grateful for the coffee plants, for the sun, for the rain. I'm grateful for the hands that picked the beans. But what about the businessman who profits handsomely from their sale? Am I grateful for a socially unjust system? I don't want my gratitude to be sentimental or politically naive.

NEVER ON VACATION from this incarnation.

I ADMIT IT: my memory isn't what it used to be. I forgot what number we're supposed to dial when we see the Supreme Court leaving the scene of a crime — for what else to call last year's 5–4 decision to kill campaign-finance reform? I don't remember why we're rounding up illegal aliens instead of the well-to-do Americans who illegally employ them. Nor can I recall exactly when President Obama promised that the next war we fight will be the most eco-friendly in history — our troops dressed in uniforms made of 100 percent organic cotton, our "green bombs" produced in factories constructed of straw bales. Maybe I heard it on National Public Radio, just before they announced that from now on all the news will be recycled, since nothing really changes, and it's wasteful to use a story just once.

OSAMA BIN LADEN IS DEAD. Do I feel safer? Not really. Do I feel more patriotic? Well, I've never been one to wave the flag — not after 9/11 and not during any of the misguided wars my country has fought and won, or fought and lost. Even with Barack Obama in office, I still feel like an outsider when Independence Day rolls around and the banners are unfurled and the weapons are counted. Still, unlike some of my friends, I haven't given up on our president. Is Obama perfect? Of course not. But is he any less skillful at leading the nation than some of my friends are at governing themselves? Are they smarter than he is? Are they more principled? When they make a New Year's resolution, do they keep it?

THE BILLS ARE PAID; my desk is neat. If God took note of such things, surely he'd be impressed. But instead he keeps asking me the same questions: Was I too busy to cry yesterday? If I cried, were my tears for myself or for another? If I wept for my brother, what made me stop and turn away?

AS CHRISTMAS APPROACHES, I'm reminded of the ice storm that knocked out electricity to hundreds of thousands of homes in North Carolina in the winter of 2002. During the week we went without power, Norma and I slept in front of our fireplace every night, huddled together for warmth. Before the week ended, I happened to drive through a neighborhood that was one of the first to get power back. When I saw a brightly lit Santa on someone's lawn, I had a momentary urge to do something unneighborly. How envious I felt. They had power and we didn't. Then I wondered: in a world where 800 million people don't have enough to eat, what's it like to feel this way every day of your life?

New and Improved Commandments

MY GREEN-EYED CAT is on my lap. My wife is still asleep down the hall. My cat is purring. My wife is snoring. I'm sixty-six years old, and my coffee's getting cold. I was born in Brooklyn in 1945. They named me "Seymour," but still I survived. I know I should be grateful just to be here today. Friends much younger have already passed away. The sky was dark before; now it's streaked with gold. I'm sixty-six years old, and my coffee's getting cold.

THERE'S ONE UNDENIABLE deadline for everything on my to-do list. Because I don't know when that deadline is, it seems less real to me than my monthly deadlines at *The Sun*. But it's unquestionably more real, as real as all the different clocks in all the different time zones agreeing on one thing: sixty minutes in an hour; twenty-four hours in a fleeting day; and one of those days will be my last, my nonnegotiable deadline. Extra time for good behavior? Fat chance. A note from my doctor insisting that a cure is just around the corner? Maybe I can hire a couple of stand-up comedians to entertain Death long enough for me to slip out the back door. But the door is locked and rigged with explosives. The sign reads: NO EXIT. TURN AROUND. FACE DEATH LIKE A MAN. Meanwhile the comedians are on a roll. Death hasn't laughed this much since Timothy Leary wanted to have his brain frozen so he could come back to life one day like a popsicle on a stick.

REMINDER TO SELF: I don't have to pretend to be anything other than a balding mammal who's still trying to lose a few pounds. I don't have to climb to the top of the mountain, then return to my people with ten new and improved commandments in my hand. Just a word or two of encouragement will do. For example, I can reliably report that wandering for forty years in the desert isn't such a big deal — not when it takes ten years to get rid of a single bad habit; twenty years to shuck another; thirty years to discover the simplest truths about what it means to love someone. I can do forty years in the desert standing on my head.

IN *A TERRIBLE LOVE OF WAR*, James Hillman writes that there have been 14,600 wars during 5,600 years of recorded history. It's worthwhile to remember this the next time I throw up my hands at the warring tribes within my psyche, or berate myself for not having realized a lasting state of inner peace.

CAN I BE GRATEFUL that I ate too much last night after Norma had gone to bed? Well, I was hungry, and I was fed. No, I didn't eat mindfully. But I was mindful enough to put the food in a bowl and lift a spoon to my lips. I can be grateful that, in a world where so many millions went to bed hungry, one man sat eating in his kitchen, his cat nearby, his wife asleep upstairs. I can be grateful for his great good fortune: the persimmon-colored bowl filled

with fruit and nuts and yogurt; the pine trees creaking
in the wind; the gravity that keeps him on this spinning
planet — all of him, every single pound of him.

THE ANIMAL BODY SAYS: Put down the book. Walk away
from the desk. The animal body says: Get down on your
knees and pray. But don't pray just to your unseen God.
Remember me. The animal body says: I am with you always. When you ignore me, I am with you, and when you
stare glumly in the mirror and still don't see me, I am with
you. The animal body says: Take all those spiritual books
and pile them high. Then climb to the top of the stack. See
how much closer you are to heaven? The animal body says:
Start with where your feet touch the ground.

My Secret Notebook

I PROMISED TO DRIVE a friend to the airport this morning, so I'm up at four. For years, I used to get up at four every morning in order to write. Now I sleep until five. To some people, five seems early. But it's not. Four is early. Four is a man who laughs in time's face; five knows better. Four speaks his mind; five thinks first. Four imagines that, if he keeps trying, someday he'll convince himself he's a real writer; five finishes this sentence and walks away.

WHEN KATSUSHIKA HOKUSAI, one of Japan's best-known artists, turned seventy-three, he said that he'd learned "a little" about painting. Just before he died at eighty-nine, he said that he might have become "a real painter" if heaven had given him ten more years.

IF A WORD COULD ONLY BE true enough. If a day could only last.

MY HANDS ARE COLD this morning. They'd rather be in bed with Norma than wrapped around this pen — but then the pen would be cold, and this page empty. Better an empty bed than an empty page, I tell myself, as if the gods will be impressed by my little sacrifice. I agree with Woody Allen that 80 percent of success is just showing up. But what about the other 20 percent? I sit here, waiting for the Muse to arrive. Sometimes she does. Sometimes she sleeps late and lets me struggle on my own.

THE MUSE FINALLY ARRIVES, without a word of apology. (But God forbid if *I'm* not here on time.) She unbuttons her blouse, slips off her skirt. *It's been so long,* I stammer. *What if I do something stupid?* She laughs. *Of course you'll do something stupid.*

MY CAT FRANNY is asleep on my desk chair, and I don't want to move her. Maybe I'll let her do my work today while I sit on the floor grooming myself, which is probably harder than it looks. Then again, so is writing sentences that move across the page on little cat feet; so is getting the English language to curl up in your lap and purr.

INSIDE MY NOTEBOOK is another notebook, so secret even I rarely see it. Sometimes when I seem to be taking a nap, or walking down a street, or bending over to tie my shoe, I'm really trying to glance inside my secret notebook.

SY SAFRANSKY

Third Planet from the Sun

NORMA LEAVES FOR FLORIDA tomorrow to spend the weekend with her family. Since our regular housesitter is out of
town, I'll be staying at home with our cats. I'll miss Norma,
but I won't miss hearing some of her relatives pillory Barack
Obama as a socialist intent on dismantling capitalism (if
only) or a closet Muslim with a bogus birth certificate.
Impassioned political debate is a beautiful thing in a democracy; at a family gathering, I'm not so sure. Fortunately
Franny and Zooey's political beliefs line up nearly perfectly
with mine, although they may be a little more patient than I
am with that cool cat in the White House, and a little to the
left of me on animal rights.

I WOKE UP THIS MORNING on the third planet from the
sun. In the second decade of the twenty-first century. In the
United States of America. Outside, the sky was still dark,
but at the flip of a switch the room was flooded with light.
Incredible!

I turned on the radio: two more U.S. soldiers killed in
Afghanistan. Now, how incredible is that? The leadership of
al-Qaeda has been decimated. Osama bin Laden has been
dispatched by an elite team of Navy seals. Yet the war in
Afghanistan drags on. More than two thousand U.S. soldiers have died there. More than seventeen thousand have
been wounded. Thousands of Taliban fighters and tens of
thousands of Afghan civilians have been killed. Operation
Enduring Freedom, military officials call it. Operation

Enduring Heartache is what it's become.

How odd to be a citizen of the most powerful nation on earth, a country that, with less than 5 percent of the world's population, spends nearly as much on defense as the rest of the world combined; a superpower that's gone to war so often during my lifetime — Germany, Japan, Korea, Vietnam, Laos, Cambodia, Grenada, Panama, Iraq, Bosnia, Afghanistan, Iraq again — you'd think it's a habit we can't break.

BEFORE LONG we'll be commemorating the fiftieth anniversary of John F. Kennedy's assassination, a dark day in American history and a turning point in my life. I know now that our country lost its innocence long before the death of our thirty-fifth president, who was hardly an innocent himself. Yes, not even John F. Kennedy was John F. Kennedy. I was only eighteen when the president was killed in 1963, and, though I was no radical, the Warren Commission's finding that Lee Harvey Oswald acted alone was about as credible to me as George W. Bush's assertion, decades later, that Iraq had stockpiled weapons of mass destruction. My naive faith in my government was shattered. Soon I began to question everything from the war in Vietnam to our numerous alliances with tyrants and torturers to our own relentless buildup of weapons of mass destruction. Everything.

MAYBE I EXPECT too much from my country. As empires go, America, you're still wet behind the ears: too much of an adolescent to stop getting into a fight every fifteen minutes; too arrogant to admit when you're wrong; unwilling to walk a mile in someone else's shoes because you're too lazy to pull over and get out of the car. How much weight did you lose on that last diet? That's what I thought. How many times have we begged you to confess that it was you who tortured the neighbor's pets? Each time, you shake your head and insist you've never tortured anyone.

HISTORY LAUGHS as the wind lifts her skirts. It's too late for modesty now.

I READ SOME NINTH-CENTURY Chinese poems to get inspired this morning, but it's not working. I'm not up there on Cold Mountain with Han Shan, in his tattered coat and worn-out sandals, waiting for the sun to burn the mist away. I'm here in North Carolina, in the twenty-first century, watching the sun rise on a world Han Shan couldn't have imagined. Then again, maybe an eccentric poet born to privilege, who chose to live in poverty, would understand the world of 2013 all too well. Maybe humanity isn't as different as we'd like to think after more than a thousand years of progress. Now, as then, political dynasties rise and fall; people squabble over money and status and power and possessions; everything changes and nothing changes. Now, as then, a boy goes to sleep at night and wakes up an old man.

Tidy Little Squares

ON MY WAY BACK from my morning run, I passed my
neighbor Ray puttering in his garden. He nodded encour-
agingly. "Sy," he called out, "you're going to live forever." I
burst out laughing. "I don't think so," I said. We talked for
a few minutes about the woman he was in love with; he
said he couldn't get over how beautiful she looked when
she smiled at him in the morning. "Maybe that's where we
live forever, Ray," I said.

W.S. MERWIN writes of our "passion for the momentary
countenance of the unrepeatable world."

HOW DOMESTICATED I've become: still married to the
same woman; a faithful companion to my two cats; a man
whose habits are very . . . habitual. I even chastise myself in
habitual ways, excoriating myself decade after decade for
the same modest sins of commission and omission: eating
too much, praying too little. Of course, all this can change
in a moment. One day it will. As a Buddhist monk in Sri
Lanka said after the 2004 South Asian tsunami: "We'll try
to explain to the people the impersonal nature of the event.
Our life doesn't belong to us; it's like a flame that can be
extinguished in an instant, without warning." The reality
of impermanence is hard to bear. Sometimes I try to shut it
out; like everyone else, I have my ways. But, paradoxically,
I feel more alive when I acknowledge that I can't know

anything about the future. *Anything*. Tomorrow is a secret the world knows how to keep.

MY WATCH STOPPED WORKING. Just like that. No warning. No letter advising me that time was about to stand still. Since it was an inexpensive watch and not worth fixing, I've hung it on the wall next to my calendar: a reminder that it's unwise to take refuge in all those tidy little squares, lined up like soldiers ready to do my bidding; that, for each of us, "next week" is merely a hypothesis.

I CAME ACROSS AN INTERVIEW with the playwright Arthur Miller conducted in 2004. Miller was eighty-nine and had a thirty-four-year-old girlfriend. He'd met her shortly after the death of his third wife, to whom he was married for forty years. The interviewer asked why a man his age would saddle himself with a new relationship and "the inevitable host of accompanying demands." Wouldn't it be easier just to call up friends when he wanted company? "Not if they're dead," Miller replied. "Then it takes longer."

DEATH IS IN NO HURRY. He'll be patiently waiting for me one night on the front steps, smoking a cigarette, looking at the stars. "Pretty evening," he'll say. I'll have to agree. Maybe I'll sit down beside him, ask for a cigarette. He'll smile. "You don't smoke," he'll say. "No," I'll reply, "but it's never too late to start."

Close Enough to Touch

WAKING IN THE DARK this morning, I'm grateful that the sun will soon be up; now, there's something I don't question, no matter how convincingly the light fled the night before. I'm grateful that Norma and I have spent most of the last ten thousand days together, even as the ice caps were melting. I'm grateful that the cats I adore are beside me, that God is sometimes close enough to touch.

HERE I AM, STILL STRUGGLING with my passions, my fears. "Lord," Saint Francis prayed, "make me an instrument of Thy peace." But do I need to become more tranquil to be an instrument of peace? Birth was a struggle; life is a struggle; dying will probably be a struggle, too. Maybe one way to be an instrument of peace is to honor the struggle, to recognize the dignity in the struggle.

I HAVEN'T MEDITATED in a while. I haven't pierced the illusion of separateness in a while. I haven't dissolved into white light in a while. I haven't taken a deep breath in a while. I haven't heard the sound of one hand clapping in a while. I haven't looked in the mirror and laughed at my disguise in a while.

I LEFT MY STORY IN A BARN so someone else could keep milking it. I left my story in the fitting room; it didn't fit me anymore. I left my story at the hospital because it wouldn't stop bleeding. I left my story at the rest stop; it needed a rest. I left my story at the body shop because it always wanted a different one. I left my story with some cash so it could never say, *Poor me*. I left my story without saying where I was going because I didn't want it to follow me; it never even noticed I was gone.

I DREAMT THAT I WAS DANCING with God. God wanted me to lead, but I was embarrassed. I dreamt that I was singing with God. God wanted me to harmonize, but I was afraid I'd sing off-key. I dreamt that God and I were smoking a joint. I was worried someone might see us. God was laughing.

ABOUT THE AUTHOR

Sy Safransky was editor of his junior-high
newspaper, his high-school newspaper, and his
college newspaper. (Guess where this is heading.)
He earned a master's degree in journalism from
Columbia University, then worked as a newspaper
reporter until he discovered that the real news
is what connects us. Twice divorced, in 1983
he married an adorable hippie who today is an
adorable psychiatrist — a good thing for him. He
has one stepson, two daughters, and three grandchildren. Miraculously, the magazine he founded
in 1974 survives to this day, but in heaven things
sometimes turn out that way.

BOOKS AVAILABLE FROM *THE SUN*

Many Alarm Clocks
Selections from Sy Safransky's Notebook.

Four in the Morning
ESSAYS BY SY SAFRANSKY
Thirty of Sy Safransky's best essays.

A Bell Ringing in the Empty Sky
THE BEST OF *THE SUN*, VOLS. I AND II
The finest interviews, short stories, essays, photographs, and poems from the first decade of *The Sun*.

Stubborn Light
THE BEST OF *THE SUN*, VOLUME III
Compelling works from *The Sun*'s second decade.

The Mysterious Life of the Heart
WRITING FROM *THE SUN* ABOUT PASSION, LONGING, AND LOVE
Some of the magazine's most talented writers explore the enigma of love.

Sunbeams
A BOOK OF QUOTATIONS
Our first collection of memorable Sunbeams from the magazine's back pages.

Paper Lanterns
MORE QUOTATIONS FROM THE BACK PAGES OF *THE SUN*
An eclectic recent collection of Sunbeams.

To order books, please visit **thesunmagazine.org/books**.

The Sun 107 N. Roberson St. Chapel Hill, NC 27516